WHEN
THE
SUN
DIES

WHEN
THE
SUN
DIES

Roy A. Gallant

MARSHALL CAVENDISH ▲ New York

ACKNOWLEDGMENT

I wish to thank Dr. Jerry LaSala, astrophysicist and chairman of the department of physics, University of Southern Maine, for his many helpful comments on reading the manuscript for this book.

Picture research: Jeannine L. Dickey

Library of Congress Cataloging-in-Publication Data
Gallant, Roy A.
When the sun dies / by Roy A. Gallant.
p. cm.   Includes bibliographical references and index.
Summary: Discusses what is known about the sun in particular and stars in general and describes some possible effects of the sun's gradual demise on life on earth.
ISBN 0-7614-5036-X   1. Sun—Juvenile literature. 2. Stars—Juvenile literature. [1. Sun. 2. Stars.] I. Title.
QB521.5.G345   1999   523.7—dc21   98-9430   CIP   AC

The text of this book is set in 11 point ITC Cheltenham.
Printed in the United States of America
First edition

6 5 4 3 2 1

FOR ANN

CONTENTS

PREFACE

WARNING: Unauthorized people are not encouraged to read this book. Such people include those who don't give a hoot about how or when our planet and all its life are scheduled to be burned to a crisp; those who aren't really interested in the day the Sun goes on a rampage and swells up as a red giant star, gobbling up Mercury and possibly Venus and Earth; those who don't care a fig about the climatic tortures Earth has endured in the past and is bound to endure many more times; those who could care less about how the Sun and their home planet were formed; those who don't think it's cool that some stars have hiccups that make them flicker and that others blow cosmic bubbles; those who think science is just a waste of time anyway; those who believe the Bible has all the answers to everything; and especially those who are bored with life and would rather just take a nap.

If you consider yourself "authorized," then . . .

COME WITH ME

- Come with me to a red star billions of times larger than Earth.
- Come with me, for we will journey inside the mysterious Sun.
- Come with me, for I know of planets where there are men who wear strange forms and who are a billion years old.
- Come with me to a planet eternally bathed with red fog.
- Come with me, for I will lead you to stars where gold is made.
- As we drift through space, I will take you through gossamer veils of stellar dust, the ash of stars that have blown themselves asunder and whose old atoms are the very vibrant ones you and I are made of.
- Come with me. I will take you on a journey through time, to yesterdays and tomorrows that you can't imagine and won't believe.

1 ▾

A HOME FOR THE SUN

STARS GALORE

On a clear night away from city lights the sky becomes a magic place. Strange and mysterious things are found there. To the unaided eye, the heavens sparkle as a thousand colored sequins are flung asunder. So wondrous is the night sky "that all the world will be in love with night," as Shakespeare sang in his play *Romeo and Juliet*.

Scattered through the seemingly endless depths of space are countless trillions of stars, sparkling blue, amber, ruby, and emerald from their secret orbs in deep space. Mile after cosmic mile they march on and on until they grow too dim to be seen by the naked eye, or even through our largest telescopes. The Hubble Space Telescope can see billions of stars. A small telescope reveals hundreds of thousands. With seven-power binoculars you can see more than 50,000 stars, and your unaided eye can pick out some 2,000 or more.

Ancient stargazers could not imagine the immensity of the stellar system we now call our galaxy, the Milky Way. Here thousands of stars are seen in the region of the Milky Way near the constellation Cygnus.
MOUNT WILSON AND LOS CAMPANAS OBSERVATORIES

Their jewel-like twinkling, called *scintillation,* is caused as their light is shaken and bent by the shimmering atmosphere.

The stars of the constellations are our cosmic neighbors. They belong to that vast city of some 300 billion stars that makes up our home galaxy, the Milky Way. The billions of other galaxies beyond our own are so distant that we see them only as fuzzy patches through binoculars. We can pick out their individual stars only with telescopes. Some of the stars in those distant galaxies serve as beacons that enable us to measure the immense distances across the Universe. Similar stars in the Milky Way are used to measure the size of our galactic home. Until recently, astronomers generally thought that all stars are gravitationally locked within their home galaxies. Not so. More often than previously believed, a star may be gravitationally flung out of its galaxy as an outcast in intergalactic space. Perhaps twenty percent of all stars are intergalactic outcasts.

The units of measure astronomers use are not miles or kilometers. They are much larger units called *light-years*. One light-year is the distance light travels through space in one year at the rate of 186,000 miles (300,000 kilometers) a second. That distance comes to some 6 trillion miles (9.6 trillion kilometers). On that scale, our nearest neighboring star, Alpha Centauri, is 4.3 light-years away, or 25 trillion miles (40 trillion kilometers). The Sun is 260,000 times closer

Our nearest galactic neighbor arranged in a gigantic spiral, like that of our home galaxy, is the Andromeda galaxy. It is nearly three million light-years distant and contains hundreds of stars. MOUNT WILSON AND LOS CAMPANAS OBSERVATORIES

than Alpha Centauri. The Sun is only about 8 light-*minutes* away, or 93 million miles (150 million kilometers); which means that it takes a particle of light 8 minutes to reach us from the Sun. Although the stars may seem packed closely together, they are not. They are candle-islands separated by unimaginably great distances. If we take the average distance between stars, and reduce the stars to the size of walnuts, the distance between them on that scale would be the distance from New York City to Chicago.

EARLY VIEWS OF THE SUN

It has been only over the past fifty or so years that we have come to learn what makes the Sun work as a star. It has been only about two hundred years since astronomers seriously began to study the Sun with powerful telescopes and other instruments. In much earlier times, the philosophers of ancient Greece could only wonder about what the Sun is made of and how it shines. Heraclitus, who lived from 540 to 475 B.C., believed that the Sun was a great hollow bowl turned upside down over Earth. Moisture from Earth, he said, rose up into the bowl, was captured and turned into flame, and made the bowl glow. At night the fires died out in the west. How all of this happened, he doesn't tell us. We cannot be too hard on the old Greek thinkers if some of their ideas seem unusual to us today. They did not have a science of chemistry to explain what the Sun is made of, or a science of physics to help them explain how the Sun shines. However, they were good mathematicians and were the first to use sound methods to measure the size and distance of the Sun and Moon.

Long before the Greeks, and long after them, many cultures assigned to the Sun the role of a creator god that held the power of life and death, and so it does, as we will find in the last chapter of this book. In Egyptian mythology life was created by the god Atum. At first, according to the story, there was only a vast ocean called Nun covering Earth. Then Atum, which means *Everything* and *Nothing,* created himself. He arose from the sea and created a small mound of earth to stand on. In old Egyptian writing the sign for this mound is ᕑᕩ. It means "to shine forth." When Atum became the ruler of creation his name changed to Atum-Ra ("Ra" means *Sun*).

Other peoples of the world have also read into the Sun the power to create life. The Yahao Chins of Burma once thought that the Sun had laid an egg from which they were hatched. And the Incas of Peru looked on the Sun as creator of the Incas and the world. The Yuchi Indians of eastern Tennessee used to call themselves People of the Sun.

Closer to our times, a curious instance in the history of astronomy involves ideas about the Sun held by one of the giants among astronomers. The British astronomer William Herschel, who lived from 1738 to 1822, reviewed all earlier studies about the Sun and tried to paint a general picture of our star. Despite its brilliance, Herschel thought that the Sun was a dark solid body like Earth and covered by two cloud layers. The outer layer, he believed, was extremely hot and bright. It was responsible for the heat we receive on Earth. The inner layer supposedly acted as a screen that protected the solid Sun below from the intense heat above. Here is what he wrote about the Sun: "Sunspots are holes [in the cloud layers] allowing us to glimpse the solid body of the Sun beneath. [That body] appears to be nothing else than a very eminent, large, and lucid planet, evidently the first, or in strictness of speaking, the only primary one of our system, all others being secondary to it." Herschel also thought that the Sun-planet was active with life. "We need not hesitate to admit that the Sun is richly stored with inhabitants," he wrote.

Considering that during Herschel's time solar astronomy had yet to be born, we should not be hard on this extraordinary man who was the finest telescope maker of his time and an expert observer. Herschel also was the first to study the orbital motions of double stars, the first person in history to discover a planet (Uranus), and the first to map a shape for the Milky Way. Any one of those achievements—let alone all four—would be enough for any man.

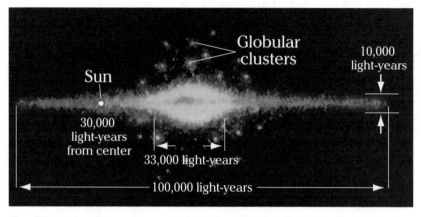

Our Milky Way galaxy is a vast collection of billions of stars in the shape of a great disk. From edge to edge it measures nearly a hundred thousand light-years. The central bulge, the nucleus, is some 33,000 light-years across. The Sun is located some 30,000 light-years from the nucleus, and the disk is a bit more than ten thousand light-years thick.

Today's solar telescopes, spectroscopes, and satellites designed to study the Sun in different kinds of light—including infrared and ultraviolet radiation, x-rays, and gamma rays—paint a very different picture of the Sun than Herschel could have imagined. As we explore the Sun and journey to its very center, try to imagine our local star as a gigantic onion made up of shells, each one wrapped closely over the one beneath, and the whole surrounded by a great cosmic halo.

2▾
THE STAR WE KNOW BEST

"Which is more important, the Sun or the Moon?" one philosopher asked another. After some thought, the second one replied, "Why, the Moon, of course, because it shines at night and gives us light. The Sun shines only during the day when it's light anyway."

THE SUN: AN "ORDINARY" STAR?

To fully appreciate our local star, we must be able to compare it with other stars. But to fully appreciate other stars astronomers first had to learn what the Sun is like—its distance from Earth, its size, how hot it is, what it is like inside, and what drives its energy-producing powerhouse that makes life on Earth possible.

The stargazers of old could only guess at the Sun's distance and size. Without a way of measuring the height of the great sky dome or the distance to the mysterious objects suspended beneath it, they could learn nothing about the size of those objects. Some 4,000 years ago the Babylonians, a Middle Eastern people who lived in a region that is now part of Iraq, built great towering holy mounds called ziggurats. The astronomer-priests of those faraway times believed that once a year the gods who ruled over the stars, Moon, and Sun assembled to discuss the affairs of humans. At such times the astronomer-priests climbed to the top of the holy mounds to communicate with the gods. If the gods inhabited the planets and stars, then those objects possibly were not so very far away. Anyone who has ever viewed the night sky on an especially clear night in the desert or high in the mountains knows the feeling of seemingly being able to reach up and touch the stars, so close do they appear.

It wasn't until the new age of mathematics in ancient Greece around 200 B.C. that astronomers seriously tried to work out the distance and size of the Sun. The first to do so was the Greek astronomer Aristarchus. He tried to measure the angle between the Sun and first-quarter Moon. Although the idea was sound in principle, the measurement was impossible to make accurately enough to calculate the Sun's actual distance from Earth. He said the Sun was twenty times more distant than the Moon, a distance far short of the Sun's actual distance. Today we know that the Sun is nearly four hundred times the Moon's distance. Even though Aristarchus's calculation was way off, it suggested that the Sun was farther away than anyone had imagined and, therefore, must be very large considering its apparent size.

About fifty years later the greatest among the astronomers of ancient times, Hipparchus, also tried to measure the Sun's distance from Earth. His method was to time the Moon's passage through Earth's shadow during a lunar eclipse. Again, although the idea is sound, the measurement is too difficult to make accurately. Hipparchus's distance came out to only nine million miles. Although ten

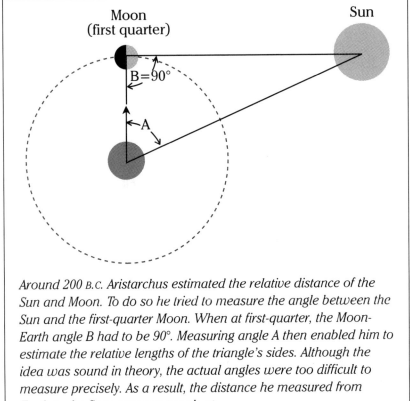

Around 200 B.C. Aristarchus estimated the relative distance of the Sun and Moon. To do so he tried to measure the angle between the Sun and the first-quarter Moon. When at first-quarter, the Moon-Earth angle B had to be 90°. Measuring angle A then enabled him to estimate the relative lengths of the triangle's sides. Although the idea was sound in theory, the actual angles were too difficult to measure precisely. As a result, the distance he measured from Earth to the Sun was way too short.

times too short, it was an improvement over Aristarchus's distance and increased the height of the great "sky dome" by an impressive amount.

Once we know the Sun's distance, we can measure its size. First we measure its apparent diameter—how wide the Sun is across a ruler held out at arm's length—and then we can compute its actual diameter. The distance across the Sun's disk turns out to be 864,000 miles (1,390,000 kilometers). That is broad enough to allow 110 Earths to be strung across the Sun's face. The Sun is large enough to stuff a million Earths inside. If we could fit the Sun on a cosmic scale, it would weigh 300,000 times more than Earth. And finally, the Sun contains more than 99.8 percent of all matter in the Solar System. Although those figures may seem impressive, they are mere drops in a bucket compared with some of the stars we will visit later in this chapter. The Sun, it turns out, is a rather ordinary star, only slightly larger than most of the stars we see.

A JOURNEY TO THE SUN'S CENTER

During a total solar eclipse, when the Moon glides by between us and the Sun, the Sun's glaring disk is all but hidden. At such times the Sun's outer diffuse layer of gas becomes visible as a great spherical halo of frail feathery cloud. Except during an eclipse, or seen from space, this layer of the Sun's outer atmosphere is too dim to shine against the blue sky. It is called the *corona.* The total amount of light cast by the corona is about half that reflected by the full Moon. Unlike other regions of the Sun, the corona swells up and shrinks from time to time. In attempts to measure its height, astronomers have found that the corona sometimes stretches more than a million miles (more than 1.6 million kilometers) from the Sun's surface.

One of the mysteries of the Sun's coronal atmosphere is how to account for its high temperature of some 2 million K. "K" stands for degrees on the Kelvin temperature scale and expresses the speed of the atoms of a gas. We enjoy a temperature of 300 K on a nice summer day, which is 81°F (27°C). Oddly enough, the Sun's coronal temperature is about 300 times higher than the Sun's surface. But the corona's high temperature on the Kelvin scale should not be confused with heat. Its atoms move fast, but its gases are so thin that they would not budge the mercury in a thermometer.

Like the rest of the Sun, the corona is made up of about 72 percent hydrogen (by weight), about 27 percent helium, and traces of carbon, nitrogen, and oxygen, as well as heavier elements such as

During a solar eclipse, the Sun's outer diffuse layer of gasses becomes visible as a great spherical halo of frail feathery cloud. Called the corona, this layer of the Sun's outer atmosphere is too dim to shine against the blue sky except during an eclipse. NASA

nickel, gold, and uranium. In general, the heavier the element, the less of it is found in the Sun.

If astronomers are not very happy about their meager knowledge of the corona, they are even less happy about their knowledge of the lower solar atmosphere, the chromosphere, which rims the Sun's "surface" gases. During an eclipse the *chromosphere,* which

The Sun is a huge ball of hydrogen gas with lesser amounts of helium and traces of all the other known chemical elements. One hundred ten Earths could fit across the Sun's diameter. The upper atmosphere is called the corona. The lower atmosphere is called the chromosphere, meaning "light sphere." A convective zone boils hot gases up to the surface. The lower radiative zone acts as a blanket that insulates the extremely hot core region where the Sun's nuclear furnace rages and produces all the energy that keeps Earth a living planet.

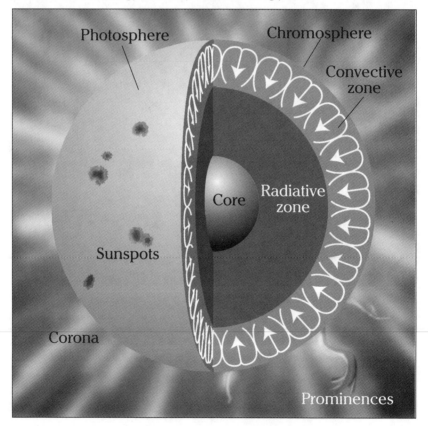

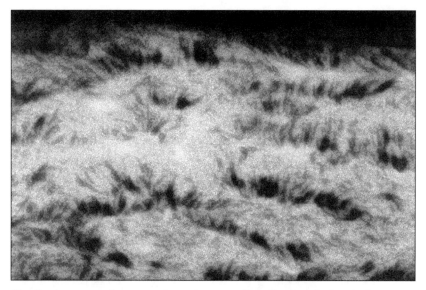

The Sun's corona has countless giant needles of gas called spicules. Like the giant cells of the photosphere, the spicules last only a few minutes before they vanish and are then replaced by new ones shot up from the denser gases below. NOAO

means "color sphere," appears as a narrow, dark red rim around the Sun. But its narrow appearance is misleading. The depth of the chromosphere may be some 8,000 or so miles (13,000 kilometers). The temperature of the chromosphere's upper region gases seems to reach some 50,000 K. The gases there are ten trillion times thinner than the air we breathe. As we descend through the chromosphere we find that the temperature falls off gradually until it is only about 4,500 K at the base. Here we also find millions of giant needles of gases, called *spicules,* surging upward. The spicules come and go as they form and dissolve, with new ones taking their place every few minutes.

If you view the Sun through dark welder's glasses you will see a sharp circular line at the bottom of the chromosphere. The line marks the outer edge of the *photosphere,* the "surface" of the Sun. *(Photos* comes from the Greek and means "light.") It might well have been this solid-appearing line that misled Herschel into thinking that a cool and solid "primary planet" was to be found within the Sun's hot gaseous cocoon. The photosphere shines at about 6,000 K, its vast store of energy welling up from deep within the solar interior. Since heat flows only in one direction—from a hot region to a cooler region—we can expect the Sun to grow increasingly hotter the deeper we go, and it does.

Since we can see only a few miles into the photosphere, our view of the Sun stops here. The photosphere-surface gases are about as dense as our air at sea level. The first hundred or so miles (160 or so kilometers) down serve as the electric light bulb for the Solar System. And what an electric light bulb it is! It shines with the brilliance of 400,000,000,000,000,000,000,000,000 watts. That amounts to 40 trillion trillion ordinary 100-watt light bulbs. To pay the light bill for only one second would cost more than the total production output of the United States over a period of 7 million years.

Photographs of the photosphere show millions of gas mounds called *granules.* They measure about four hundred miles (650 kilometers) across their bright rounded tops, and their roots go hundreds to thousands of miles deep. The nineteenth-century astronomer A. Secchi compared the mounds to "grains of rice bubbling in a milky fluid." The granules are in continuous motion, forming, dissolving, and reforming about every five minutes. As a new granule boils up, its hot top quickly cools and darkens. The cooled gases then fall back down into the Sun, are reheated, and rise again as new bright granules. The result is that the entire surface of the photosphere is a checkerboard of bright, rising hot cells of gas interspersed with cool, sinking dark cells.

The rising and falling gas cells of the photosphere cause the Sun to pulse every five minutes. For 2.5 minutes it puffs up as the hot

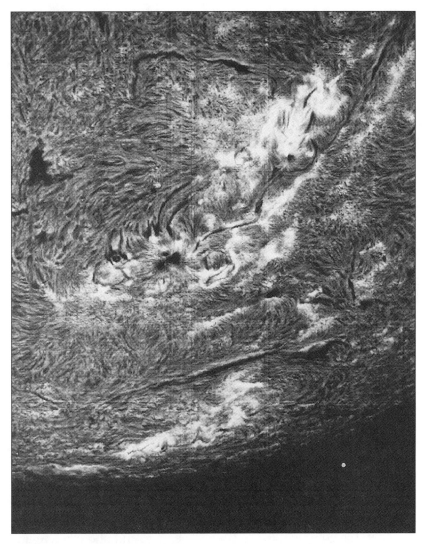

The Sun's photosphere "surface" has countless cells of gases continuously forming, dissolving, and forming again. As a hot and bright gas cell, or granule, rises to the surface, it cools and darkens before collapsing and dissolving. A typical granule is some four hundred miles (650 kilometers) across and lasts about five minutes. MOUNT WILSON AND LAS CAMPANAS OBSERVATORIES cells rise, then over the next 2.5 minutes it shrinks as the cool cells fall. Remarkably, the pulsing action is caused by sound waves that make the entire Sun ring like a huge, deep-toned bell gonging a strange solar symphony. A network of solar astronomers around the world devote their time to studying our noisy Sun and its oscillations. Their group is aptly named GONG, standing for Global Oscillation Network Group. Sound waves in the Sun travel at different speeds, depending on the density and temperature of the gases they pass through. Because they do, the Sun's sound waves can be used to find out about density, temperature, composition, and motions in the Sun's interior.

In 1997 a satellite named SOHO (Solar and Heliospheric Observatory) launched in 1995 to study the Sun surprised astronomers with unexpected findings. For one, the Sun has a jet stream of hot gases circling its north polar region.

Beneath the photosphere is a region called the *convective zone.* Giant conveyor-like cells of gas carry heat from a depth of 124,000 miles (200,000 kilometers) up to the base of the photosphere and so keep it hot. Between the bottom of the convective zone and the outer edge of the Sun's central core is a region called the *radiative zone.* Here the temperatures rise to hundreds of thousands and then millions of degrees, and the gas pressure climbs unimaginably high. The gases become as dense as water, then denser than slush, and finally much denser than concrete. The radiative zone serves the Sun in two ways: Its dense gases act as an insulating blanket that keeps the fiercely hot core from cooling down; and it transports the energy produced in the core up into the convective zone and photosphere and then to the outside.

Beneath the radiative zone and forming a ball at the Sun's center is the core, burning at some 15,000,000 K. Its gases are ten times denser than gold. The core is the immense nuclear furnace that runs the solar heat factory. But heat and light are only two forms of the energy emitted by the Sun. It pours out energy all along the *electromagnetic spectrum.* That energy ranges from the highly damaging gamma rays at one extreme to the much less energetic radio waves at the other extreme.

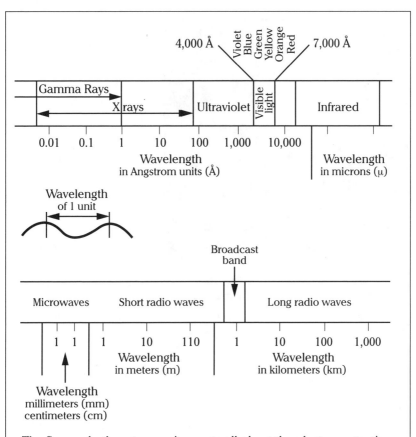

The Sun and other stars emit energy all along the electromagnetic spectrum. At one end is the highly damaging gamma radiation. At the opposite end are radio waves. By observing stars, nebulae, and other matter of the Universe through the energy "windows" of the electromagnetic spectrum, astronomers learn about what the Universe is made of and how it behaves.

STORMS ON THE SUN

In addition to its acoustic feat of ringing like a gigantic gong, the Sun puts on spectacular visual displays that we often feel on Earth.

SUNSPOTS were first observed through a telescope by the Italian astronomer Galileo in 1610. But naked-eye sightings of especially large sunspots were made as early as about 300 B.C. They range from a few hundred to many thousands of miles across. We see them in pairs as dark craters a few hundred miles deep in the photosphere. Exactly what causes them is not well understood, but we have several clues.

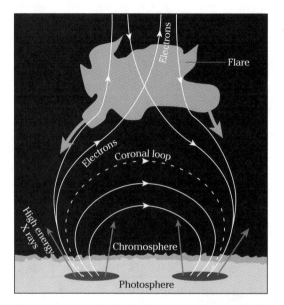

Sunspots appear in the Sun's photosphere as dark craters a few hundred miles deep and hundreds to thousands of miles across. They occur in pairs and seem to be formed by gigantic magnetic loops generated deep within the Sun. When the magnetic lines become twisted, they may trigger violent storms called solar flares.

As the Sun rotates on its axis, its gases at the equator are carried around faster than gases at the poles. Since the sunspots are embedded in the photosphere gases, they too are carried around. As gases within the Sun are swirled in one direction by the Sun's rotation, they are also carried upward and downward by the motion of the convective zone. These motions bend the Sun's magnetic field in such a way that several small magnetic fields form. Shaped like horseshoe magnets, they stick out of the Sun like croquet wickets, looping up out of the photosphere, arcing high into the corona, and then looping back down again. At the base of each magnetic loop is a pair of sunspots. Sunspots come and go in cycles of eight to fifteen years, averaging very nearly eleven years. But this eleven-year activity cycle is actually half of a twenty-two-year solar magnetic cycle. The chart shows the history of sunspot activity since the year 1620.

When the Sun is especially active it breaks out with many sunspots. Since the spots are large and dark, we might at first expect the Sun to dim somewhat during its active sunspot periods. Instead, it becomes brighter! The brightening is caused by the outbreak of fiery patches in the photosphere called *faculae,* Latin for "little torches." So as sunspot activity increases about every eleven years, so does faculae activity. The brightening action of the faculae overpowers the dimming action of the sunspots.

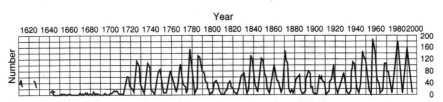

The graph shows a succession of peak periods of an active Sun from about 1620 to 1998. Sometimes there is a span of only eight years between peak periods, other times as long as seventeen years. Few sunspots were reported for the fifty year period from 1650 to 1700. AFTER J. EDDY

PROMINENCES AND FLARES Before sunspots break out they are often announced days ahead of time by the sudden appearance of other solar storms. Among them are enormous streamers of fiery gas shooting out to a height of 500,000 miles (800,000 kilometers) or more. These solar prominences often outlive the sunspots by days, weeks, or even months.

Spikelike projections called surges join the solar display by darting straight up out of the Sun. Other prominences form lazy fiery loops of gas, and still others appear as great luminous clouds. Flares are among the most dramatic and violent solar storms. Lasting only a minute or so, they are immense flashes of gasses at 20,000,000 K or more. They explode out of the corona, usually between sunspot pairs. In addition to all this activity, the Sun continuously sends out streams of protons and electrons that sweep through the Solar System as the *solar wind.*

Whenever there is an outburst of solar activity we can expect magnetic storms that interfere with short wave radio signals and that can damage the electronics in communications and other satellites. In August 1989 a solar outburst temporarily shut down the computers of the Toronto Stock Exchange. When the solar wind kicks up from time to time, swarms of protons and electrons are caught up in Earth's magnetic field, flow down into the upper atmosphere at the North and South Poles, and cause spectacular displays of northern lights. These particles are also thought to disrupt the magnetic navigation abilities of migrating birds, and to set compass needles quivering.

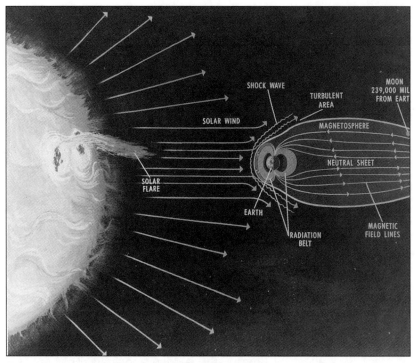

A continuous stream of protons and electrons pour out of the Sun and sweep through the solar system as the solar wind. As the solar wind strikes Earth's magnetic field, it compresses the field on the sunward side and stretches it out on the opposite side. The solar wind triggers magnetic storms that sometimes disrupt electronics equipment, including communications satellites. NASA

How the Sun Produces Energy

In one second the Sun emits more energy than people have used on this planet ever since there have been people. In only one minute the Sun could melt an eleven-mile- (eighteen-kilometer-) thick layer of ice. Fortunately Earth receives only a tiny fraction (0.000,000,000,005 percent) of that energy. Otherwise, our planet would be cooked in an instant. How does the Sun produce its staggering amount of energy?

Around 1848 J. R. Mayer guessed that millions of meteorites continuously crashed into the Sun and so kept it hot and made it shine. But his idea was abandoned when it couldn't explain why Mercury,

Venus, and Earth had long been targeted by meteorites but were not similarly heated.

Six years later the German scientist Hermann von Helmholtz said that maybe the Sun produces its energy by shrinking and so compacting its gases in a hot squeeze. Such a contracting object would, in fact, produce energy. But it turned out that in order for the Sun to produce its tremendous energy output by contraction, a shrinking Sun could last only 30 million years before shrinking away

Fiery loops of gas leap hundreds of thousands of miles into the solar sky from time to time, as seen in this photograph taken during a solar eclipse. Most of the gases fall back into the Sun, but some escape off into space. MOUNT WILSON AND LAS CAMPANAS OBSERVATORIES

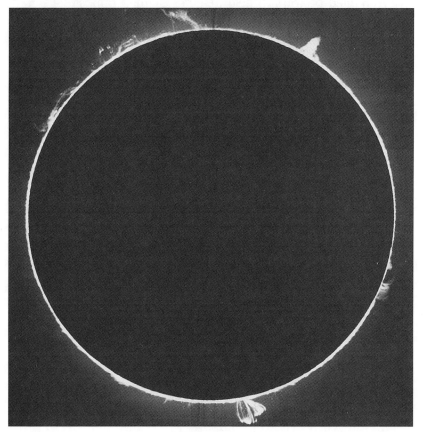

to nothing. Later, when geologists showed that the fossil record went back more than 500 million years, von Helmholtz's idea also had to be abandoned.

Then came the year 1939 when Hans Bethe, Carl von Weizsäcker, George Gamow, and others came up with a new Sun-burning theory, the one that seems to work very well to this day and that just about all astronomers accept. The Sun's energy factory is in its dense core region, they said, and it is fueled by the Sun's vast store of hydrogen. The lightest of the more than a hundred chemical elements, the hydrogen atom has one particle called a *proton* forming the center, or *nucleus,* of the atom. It also has a much less massive particle called an *electron* moving about in a shell surrounding the nucleus. At room temperature the negatively charged electron and the positively charged proton are held together by their opposite electrical charges. But inside the Sun things are different enough to upset this tidy arrangement. The tremendous heat and pressure there move the atoms about so fast that they collide forcefully and knock their electrons out of orbit. As a result, there is a sea of free-swimming electrons and free-swimming protons all mixed up.

If the temperature in the core of a star is less than about 7,000,000 K, the free-swimming electrons and protons don't do much of anything. The plus electrical charges of the protons act as invisible energy bumpers that prevent the protons from sticking together. This is similar to the like ends of two bar magnets pushing each other away. When two protons collide they just bounce off one another, like two billiard balls. But when the tremendous mass of a star's outer gases is pulled down toward the core region by gravity, the core matter is crushed with tremendous force. When the gravitational infall of those gases pushes the core temperature above 7,000,000 K something interesting begins to happen to the protons. They are now darting about so fast and colliding so vigorously that their invisible energy bumpers no longer work. The two protons may then fuse into a single lump of matter, as shown on page 34. As they do, one of the protons is changed into a *neutron,* a particle with no electric charge at all. During the change, a particle called a *positron* is created. At the same time something called a *neutrino* also is created. I say "something" because neutrinos are very mysterious.

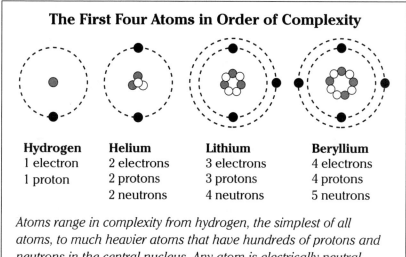

The First Four Atoms in Order of Complexity

Hydrogen	Helium	Lithium	Beryllium
1 electron	2 electrons	3 electrons	4 electrons
1 proton	2 protons	3 protons	4 protons
	2 neutrons	4 neutrons	5 neutrons

Atoms range in complexity from hydrogen, the simplest of all atoms, to much heavier atoms that have hundreds of protons and neutrons in the central nucleus. Any atom is electrically neutral when the number of negatively-charged electrons matches the number of positively-charged protons. The Sun's fierce heat strips electrons away from atoms.

We might pause here for a word about those fascinating particles. Astronomers don't know very much about them, but what they do know is rather interesting because it is so unusual. Try to imagine a "particle" that doesn't have any mass, or matter. Ordinary matter like concrete, lead, and you, for instance, means nothing to neutrinos. They travel at the speed of light, and nothing seems to stop them—well, practically nothing. It would take a wall of lead about three trillion miles (4.8 trillion kilometers) thick to stop one. Every second, 66 billion neutrinos from the Sun whiz through each patch of Earth's surface the size of a baking pan—including you—and right out through the other side. These mysterious little massless particles are teaching astronomers about what goes on deep inside the Sun, and about matter itself. But let's return to where we left two colliding protons in step one of the proton-proton chain of energy production.

To complete the first step, the positron particle created when two protons fuse collides with a free-swimming electron. That collision produces two gamma rays. So a tiny amount of hydrogen mass has been changed into two bursts of gamma ray energy and one neutrino. What happens next? If you follow the next two steps in the

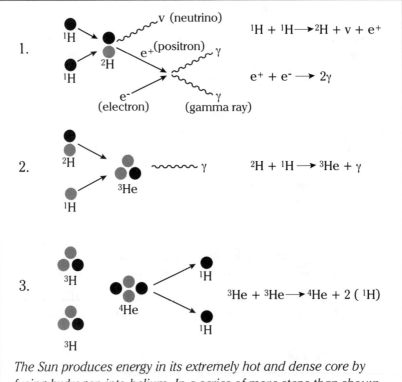

The Sun produces energy in its extremely hot and dense core by fusing hydrogen into helium. In a series of more steps than shown here, free protons (hydrogen nuclei) collide, fuse, and eventually build the nuclei of helium. At each step in the chain of reactions, energy is emitted. See text for detailed explanation.

diagram, you find that eventually the nucleus of one atom of ordinary helium (^{4}He) is built up. The energy released by all those trillions of trillions of fusion reactions going on every second in the Sun's core then takes about a million years to work its way up through the radiative zone, then through the convective zone, and finally out through the photosphere and into space. Once in space, the energy speeds to Earth in only eight minutes. The neutrinos, however, zip right up through the Sun as if it weren't even there.

So the Sun produces all its energy by burning up some of its mass as it fuses hydrogen into helium. Along the complex chain of fusion reactions energy is released. Hydrogen mass is continuously being changed into energy. That, in simple terms, is how virtually all stars produce energy and shine.

If we think about this process for a moment, we might have cause for concern. Each minute of the day and night the Sun is losing mass by converting its hydrogen fuel into energy. The question we must now ask is this: How much longer can the Sun keep shining and producing energy before it runs out of usable hydrogen fuel? A star such as the Sun would have collected enough mass when it was formed to last for about ten billion years. The Sun has been shining more or less as we see it shine today for almost five billion years. So the Sun is halfway through its life span and has another five billion years to go before changing its life-style dramatically. But what about other stars? Were all stars formed at the same time, and will all go out at the same time? What are those many other stars like? Earlier we said that most stars are Sunlike stars but a bit smaller. What about all those stars out there that are not Sunlike stars? Let's have a look at them before we resume our story of the Sun, and its family of planets.

3 ▾
STARS GREAT AND SMALL

If all stars are not just like the Sun, then what are those other stars like? Among the several thousand stars we can see through binoculars on any clear night are stars in midlife, such as the Sun. Some of those midlife stars are yellow, others blue, and still others red. There are also stars in the last throes of old age. Most such stars are white. There are stars just beginning to shine with a dull red light, and stars in the process of being born. There are giant blue stars with surface temperatures thousands of times hotter than the Sun's and small red stars only half as hot. And one day, given enough time, there will be burned-out relics of stars whose nuclear furnaces shut down in times too long ago to remember. They are destined to become dark hulks barely warm to the touch, and ultimately cold dark objects called *black dwarfs*. And there are stars that explode violently, stars that suddenly cast off shells of their gases that glow as colorful cosmic rings that could encircle the entire Solar System. And there are still other exotic stars so dense that a single teaspoon of their matter weighs more than a million tons.

For an unknown number of centuries astronomers have spent countless nights observing the night sky in the chilling air of remote mountaintops the world over. More recently they have also spent untold hours constructing stellar models on computers, all in an attempt to make sense out of the often bewildering diversity of sizes, colors, temperatures, and behaviors of stars.

THE BIRTH OF STARS

As they have since the beginning of time, stars are still forming today across the Universe. Before the age of telescopes no one could know where stars came from. Then *nebulae* were discovered. They are unimaginably huge clouds of gas and dust, such as those that block our view of the brilliant center of our home galaxy and that we observe in most other galaxies. *(Nebula* is Latin for "cloud.") The gas is mostly hydrogen with a sprinkling of helium. The "dust" consists of clumps of atoms that form more than a hundred different substances. They include water, the alcohol ethanol, methane (marsh gas), and several other carbon and oxygen compounds. Some of the dust grains are microscopic bits of rock dust coated with ices of ammonia and methane. Others are tiny grains of diamond forged by shock waves that smash carbon atoms together. Many such bits of diamond have been found in meteorites.

In the 1780s the French astronomer Charles Messier cataloged 103 nebulae. He called them "bothersome objects" because they often blocked his view. Today we look on the nebulae as treasure chests of information about how stars are born. We know of nowhere else to look for the birthplace of stars. In recent years the Hubble Space Telescope has captured incredibly beautiful images of

Stars are formed out of the gas and dust of space, within those massive clouds of matter called nebulae. A star begins its life as an especially dense blob of matter called a globule. Many are visible in this photograph of the Eagle nebula, some seven thousand light-years away, as photographed by the Hubble Space Telescope. NASA

these "stellar nurseries," as they have come to be called.

Only some fifty years ago astronomers didn't know what determined the kind of life a newly forming star would lead—whether the new star would evolve as a dwarf or a giant, whether it would have a long quiet life, or only a relatively brief one before annihilating itself in a catastrophic explosion. Today we know that the single most important property that determines a star's personality is *mass,* or the amount of matter it manages to collect when it forms. It grows in mass by gravitationally gobbling up gas and dust in whatever corner of a nebula the star happens to form.

LANDS OF THE DWARFS

There are three general classes of stars: 1) the long-lived red dwarfs; 2) intermediate-mass stars like the Sun with shorter life spans; and 3) the short-lived blue giants. The red dwarfs still pose a number of mysteries. Although there must be many of them out there, they are too faint to be seen easily, or at all. The red dwarfs are feeble energy producers because of their low mass of only about one-tenth that of the Sun. Such low mass means that the infall of gases does not build up a high enough pressure in the core to push the temperature there much above 7,000,000 K to 10,000,000 K. That is barely hot enough

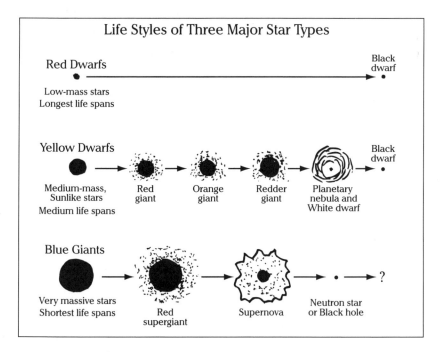

Life Styles of Three Major Star Types

Red Dwarfs

Low-mass stars
Longest life spans

Black dwarf

Yellow Dwarfs

Medium-mass, Sunlike stars
Medium life spans

Red giant

Orange giant

Redder giant

Planetary nebula and White dwarf

Black dwarf

Blue Giants

Very massive stars
Shortest life spans

Red supergiant

Supernova

Neutron star or Black hole

?

to start and maintain the proton-proton chain of nuclear reactions that fuse hydrogen into helium and so make the star shine.

These fifty-watt lightbulb stars are called red dwarfs because their low mass makes them small, and because their low core temperatures make them feeble and dim energy producers. So little energy works its way out of the core to the star's surface that the surface gases glow with a cool red light at 3,000 K, only half the Sun's surface temperature. A star's color begins to take on a special importance when we realize that color tells us the temperature of the star's surface gases. In turn the temperature of the surface gases can be an important clue to what is happening inside the star.

Color and temperature go hand in hand, as you know if you have ever watched a blacksmith heat a piece of iron. At first the iron glows red at a temperature of 1500 K; then soft yellow at about 6000 K; white at 10,000 K; and bluish white at about 50,000 K. The red stars have the lowest surface temperatures, the yellow-white stars are hotter, the white stars still hotter, and the bluish white stars the hottest.

The slow-burning nuclear furnace in the core of red dwarfs gives these stars the longest life spans. Although they have less usable hydrogen to burn than a Sunlike star has, they burn what little they have slowly. The red dwarfs may shine on for a trillion years before their nuclear fires die and the stars end their lives as cool black dwarfs. Every red dwarf star ever formed in our galaxy is still shining today. Their trillion-year life span is far longer than the age of the Galaxy itself.

A number of red dwarfs are close enough to be visible. Our closest stellar neighbors beyond the Sun are examples. They are Alpha Centauri and Proxima Centauri. Proxima Centauri shines so feebly that it would take 13,000 stars like it to equal the energy output of the Sun. With a diameter of only 40,000 miles (64,400 kilometers), it is only half the size of Jupiter. One of the most famous red dwarfs is van Biesbroeck's Star, which was discovered in 1943. Found in the constellation Aquila the Eagle it is so faint that it prompted Edward Upton to write this limerick about it:

> Van Biesbroeck's Star is so faint
> It's either a star or it ain't.
> There has even been talk
> That it's only a rock
> Covered with luminous paint.

The Hubble Space Telescope not too long ago spotted a dwarf star of a class that had existed only in theory. Called *brown dwarfs*, these stars have so little mass that their cores are unable to heat up enough to start fusing hydrogen. As a result, they are heated only by the crushing force of their gases by gravity, and they glow with a cool, brownish red light. There must be millions of these near-miss stars out there shining so faintly that we will spot one only rarely, at least until some new method of observing them comes along. One such brown dwarf is a companion of van Biesbroeck's Star, van Biesbroeck 8B. Its closeness of only twenty light-years helped its discovery.

Most stars are probably from about one-tenth as massive as the Sun to ten times more massive. Although the range in stellar mass is small, the range in size is enormous. But there is a limit to bigness. For instance, a star with a mass a hundred times greater than the Sun's would be dangerously unstable. It would shine itself apart by blowing its gases off into space. Most stars, except for the red dwarfs, at one or more times in their lives actually do cast off huge amounts of gases to space.

A red dwarf spends its trillion or so years shining by fusing hydrogen into helium. Then when its usable hydrogen is gone the star slowly dims and eventually goes out. Stars of medium mass, such as those in the Sun's class, get more out of their hydrogen fuel supply by burning hotter.

When a Sunlike star exhausts its usable hydrogen, it is left with a core of helium, for a while at least. The core temperature then falls off, as does pressure in the core. The loss of heat and pressure allows gravity to take over, and the outer layers of gas tumble down onto the core. The star collapses in on itself. The collapse once again heats the core and drives the pressure even higher than before. The helium in the core now becomes fuel and is fused into carbon. Fusion reactions in stars with masses no greater than that of the Sun cannot be pushed beyond carbon. Their fate in old age is to swell up explosively as *red giants,* and then shrink as they cool down, and finally turn into objects called *white dwarfs,* no larger than Earth. For billions of years the white dwarfs shine as intensely bright objects, but over untold billions more they grow ever cooler until eventually they fade from view as black dwarfs. But like the red dwarfs, the cooling of the white dwarfs is so slow that every white dwarf that has ever existed in the Universe is probably still shining.

This has been only a brief outline of what happens to medium-mass stars like the Sun as they evolve through several stages. Actually they swell up into red giants at least twice before ending their lives and becoming white dwarfs. We will come back to those stages in the final chapter when we describe in detail how the Sun is destined to end its life. For now, let us move on to those most spectacular of all stars—the giants and supergiants.

LANDS OF THE GIANTS

The importance of the amount of mass a star manages to scoop up gravitationally when it is born becomes dramatically evident in giant stars. And what we are learning about these stars should sharpen our appreciation of the Sun as a gentle and reliable parent of its family of planets.

The most massive stars, and some of the largest, are the blue and white giants and supergiants. Among the many we know are Rigel in the constellation Orion the Hunter; Deneb, in Cygnus the Swan; and the beautiful bluish stars in the winter star group, the Pleiades.

The blue and white giants may be hundreds of times larger and more massive than the Sun. And they may blaze away with many thousands of times more light and other energy. Their surface gases can be more than eight times the Sun's temperature, and their core temperatures may blaze away at more than 20,000,000 K. The supergiant star Mu Cephei, in the constellation Cepheus, is so large that if the star replaced our Sun it would fill the Solar System all the way out to Saturn. That makes the star more than a thousand times larger than the Sun. A billion Suns could be poured into Mu Cephei. In 1997 astronomers using the Hubble Space Telescope spotted the most energetic star known. Called the Pistol Star, it lies off toward the center of the Galaxy in the direction of the constellation Sagittarius and at a distance of 25,000 light-years. Its energy output, not its size, is the amazing thing about this star, which would easily fill Earth's orbit. In only six seconds the Pistol Star unleashes as much energy as the Sun does in a year. Some two hundred times more massive than the Sun, the young star is from one to three million years old.

The cores of these giant stars are factories that churn out all the known chemical elements. Whereas Sunlike stars fuse hydrogen into helium and then helium into carbon, the cores of the giant stars are so hot that they fuse carbon into iron. But that is the limit. No known star can fuse elements heavier than iron through the normal fusion process. But some stars do produce those heavier elements in a very different way. Let's have a look at these *T. rex* monster stars called *supernovae.*

SUPERNOVAE: STARS THAT SELF-DESTRUCT

Just to the upper right of the star marking the lower horn tip of Taurus the Bull is a faint fuzzy patch that is easily seen through a small telescope. It was discovered in 1731 and has become one of the most studied nebulae in the sky. It is the famous Crab Nebula, the remains of a hot superstar that blew itself to bits. All that was left of the star was its extremely hot exposed core.

Supernova explosions are among the most violent events we have ever witnessed in the Universe. Gamma ray bursts are even more violent, however. On December 14, 1997 astronomers observed a gamma ray explosion 100 times more violent than a supernova. Chinese astronomers saw the Crab event, recording it on July 4, 1054. They said that the "guest star," as they called it, "was visible in the day like Venus, with pointed rays in all four directions. The color was reddish white. . . It was seen altogether for twenty-three days [as a daytime object]."

The explosion may also have been recorded by at least two American Indian groups. Drawings of what seem to be the supernova have been found in northern Arizona on a wall of Navajo Canyon and in a cave at White Mesa. The clue that the drawn object may be the Crab supernova is its position beside a crescent moon, which we know was visible when that explosion was observed.

The Chinese records give us a pretty good idea of what people of the time must have seen. When the star exploded, it shone with the light of 400 million Suns for a few weeks. At a distance of some 6,300 light-years, the explosion sent a cloud of gas speeding outward at about 1,000 miles (1,600 kilometers) a second. The cloud today—the Crab Nebula—is nearly ten light-years across and still spreading out.

Supernova explosions seem to be rare events. Over the past thousand years fewer than a half dozen have been observed in our galaxy. A supernova explosion may be so bright that it outshines the combined brightness of all the stars in a galaxy. In August 1937 a supernova exploded in the galaxy IC 4182, becoming a hundred times brighter than the galaxy itself. In all, some hundred or so supernovae have been recorded in our and other galaxies.

*The Crab Nebula in the constellation Taurus the Bull is an expanding
cloud of gas, the remains of a supernova stellar explosion observed by
Chinese astronomers in the year 1054.* MOUNT WILSON AND LAS CAMPANAS
OBSERVATORIES

How can a star generate such enormous amounts of energy? In
only a few seconds it tears itself to bits with more energy than the star
had emitted over the hundreds of thousands of years of its earlier life.
Let's imagine a blue giant star with thirty times more mass than the
Sun. On exhausting its hydrogen fuel, the star switches to its helium
fuel tank and fuses oxygen and carbon. It next taps that fuel reserve
and fuses the element silicon. And finally it fuses the silicon into iron.

Since no more fusions can take place, the core begins to cool and the core pressure falls off. This permits a catastrophic collapse of the upper regions of the star. In only a second or so the infall of matter explodes away all of the star except the core of mostly iron along with some nickel. During that explosion all chemical elements heavier than iron are forged—among them gold, silver, and uranium. The cast-off cloud becomes a veil of heavy elements that floats across space at thousands of miles a second. For reasons we will find in the next chapter, the Sun and its planets were fortunate enough to meet up with just such a supernova cloud when the Sun was being formed. The exposed core of the supernova may take a year or so to dim significantly. Then it will take several years more to dim enough so that it fades from view. Supernovae are the terrorists among stars.

If we follow the fate of the iron-nickel core of a burnt-out supernova, we discover a still different class of stars. Astronomers living before 1932 couldn't even have imagined such stars, for the story of the atom and its various parts was still in its infancy and largely untold. The iron core of a supernova is so hot—billions of K—and under such great pressure that the iron nuclei are crushed into free-swimming electrons, protons, and neutrons. The electrons and protons fuse and become neutrons. Since neutrons do not have an electrical charge, there is nothing to prevent them from being squeezed extremely close together. Because the core is now a thick soup of neutrons, gravity causes a further collapse, and the core is further crushed to an object only about twenty miles (thirty kilometers) in diameter. Its matter is so dense that a teaspoon of it weighs not a million but a billion tons. The object has become a *neutron star.* By comparison, a white dwarf might seem like a ball of cotton. Some 50,000 neutron stars could be lined up across the Sun's diameter.

The gravitational collapse of a neutron star increases the spinning rate of the already spinning star, in much the same way an ice skater spins faster and faster as she draws her arms in closer and closer to her body. This effect has the important-sounding name "conservation of angular momentum." Hot spots at the magnetic poles of some of these stars emit beams of radio waves. Such stars are called *pulsars* because of their radio pulses. As a pulsar spins around, its hot spots send out signals much as the rotating light of a lighthouse does. One of the fastest pulsars found to date spins about a thousand times a second. Pulsars were first discovered in 1967. The object at the Crab nebula's center is a pulsar.

Some especially massive neutron stars collapse to about thirty-seven miles (sixty kilometers) in diameter. But how small they crunch down to depends on their mass. Less massive objects collapse to even smaller sizes. When such a star collapses beyond the neutron star stage, it just keeps collapsing forever. The object becomes so dense and its gravity so strong that no energy, not even light, can escape from it. The object has become a *black hole.*

OTHER EXOTIC STARS

Many stars go through cycles of bright to dim and back to bright as if they can't make up their minds how to shine. Called *variable stars,* more than 25,000 have been listed. It now seems that most stars probably go through one or more variable stages sometime during their lives. The Sun, as we will find later, is no exception.

Many variables pulse rhythmically and pretty much on schedule. Most pulsating variables are of the Mira type, named after the star Mira, a red giant star in the constellation Cetus the Whale. Mira-type variables have periods of about three hundred days, meaning it takes them that long to complete one cycle of going from dim to bright and back to dim again. At its brightest, the variable is about fifteen times brighter than it is when dimmest. Mira is one of the ten largest stars we can see. It normally has a diameter about four hundred times greater than the Sun, but it periodically swells up to five hundred times the Sun's diameter. The cool red gases of Mira variables burn at a temperature ranging from about 1,900 K to 2,600 K. What makes these variables swell up and shrink in fairly predictable periods is still pretty much of a mystery. One theory is that these stars are in advanced old age. They may have reached the stage when their hydrogen fuel supply has nearly run out and the fusion of hydrogen into helium has slowed. The stars may have begun to switch over to fusing helium into carbon as a source of energy production.

Another class of variable stars is the RR Lyrae variables, named after the first such variable star discovered in the year 1901 in the constellation Lyra the Harp. We know of some three thousand in the Milky Way. The stars are yellow-white giants with periods of from six to eighteen hours. A typical RR Lyra variable may double in brightness in less than half an hour, then fade back to dim in about four hours. All such stars are from fifty to sixty-five times brighter than the Sun and about six to seven times its diameter. Because the intrinsic brightness of these variables is known, and because they are sprinkled throughout the Galaxy, they have been used as yardsticks to measure the size of the Galaxy.

Still another important class of variables is the Cepheid variables. They are named after the first such star observed in 1784 in the constellation Cepheus the King. All are hot white and yellow giants with tightly scheduled periods that can often be measured down to a fraction of a second. Their periods range from a few hours up to about fifty days, but most are from five to eight days. The stars may be a stage in life between the young blue giant stars and the much older red giants.

Brighter than the RR Lyrae variables, the Cepheids can be detected in distant galaxies. Again, since their intrinsic brightness is known, and since they are commonly seen in galaxies beyond our own, they, too, can be used as yardsticks to measure the distance to those remote galaxies. In 1924 Edwin Hubble used Cepheids to discover the distance to the Andromeda Galaxy, some 2.9 million light-years away.

Some variable stars come in surprising packages. There are erupting variables with cosmic hiccups, such as the star named SS Cygni in the constellation Cygnus the Swan. This class of eruptive variables are blue dwarfs that several times a year swell up and become a hundred or so times brighter than usual. Then after a few days, they slowly fade to their usual brightness. Such stars seem to be members of double star systems, in which two stars are gravitationally locked together and orbit about each other. The more massive of such a star pair may pull surface gases off its neighbor. Those collected gases then fuel the eruption of the eruptive variable star.

Another group of variable stars that puzzle astronomers are called flash stars. There are about a half dozen of them in the Pleiades group. They flash into brightness and may remain bright from a few minutes up to three hours. Some astronomers think that the stars may be new stars in the process of heating up but not yet hot enough for their nuclear furnaces to ignite.

On the night of June 8, 1918 a star in the constellation Aquila the Eagle flared up as a *nova,* meaning "new"star. But such stars are not really new. The star had exploded and blasted off several gas shells. In only a few hours it became the brightest star, except for Sirius, in the northern sky. Before, the star had been too dim to be seen without a telescope. By the end of the month Nova Aquilae was barely visible again. Today the star is a hot, bluish dwarf smaller than the Sun.

In 1997 astronomers using NASA's Hubble Space Telescope were surprised to find that some nova outbursts do not produce smooth shells of gas, but thousands of gaseous blobs, each the size of the Solar System. This surprising discovery was made when Hubble's cameras photographed nova T Pyxidis, which erupts about every twenty years. While telescopes on the ground see a smooth shell, Hubble saw a collection of more than two thousand gaseous blobs packed into a region one light-year across. According to astronomer

Michael M. Shara of the Space Telescope Science Institute, "This observation suggests that shells of other novae do the same thing as recently ejected material plows into older, fossil material from earlier explosions."

Like eruptive variables, nova stars seem to feed off companion stars by drawing away some of their surface hydrogen gas. As the hydrogen builds up on the nova star's surface, it becomes hotter and denser until it detonates like a colossal hydrogen bomb. The explosion leads to a million-fold increase in brightness in only a day. The nova then quickly fades in several days or weeks as the hydrogen is exhausted and blown off into space. A nova explosion may be equal to a blast of 100 billion billion tons of dynamite. Most nova stars spend 10,000 to 100,000 years collecting enough hydrogen from a neighbor to ignite an explosion. But the nova known as WZ, in the constellation Sagitta the Arrow, has been seen to explode three times, once in 1913, again in 1946, and most recently in 1978.

The great gas bubble, or shell, cast off by a nova looks like a donut rather than the shell it is. That is because we look through a greater thickness of the shell's gas out around the edge. Such donut rings of expelled gases are known as *planetary nebulae*, although they have nothing to do with planets. Astronomers in the 1700s mistook these stars for planets within the Solar System. In its dying years the Sun is destined to cast off a planetary nebula ring of matter.

We could spend many more pages describing the antics of the circus performers of the cosmos—dwarfs, giants, the terrorist supernovae, and hiccupping variables among them. But knowing at least the basics about what they are made of, how their collection of mass shapes their lives, and how the nuclear activities in their cores make them behave, we are in a better position to take up the story of the Sun. We will now take a more detailed look at the matter and forces that formed it, and that formed its family of planets. To do so we turn the clock back some 4.6 billion years.

The Ring Nebula in the constellation Aquarius the Water Bearer is an example of a planetary nebula, although these nebulae have nothing to do with planets. Actually a great sphere-cloud of gas expelled by an exploding star, they appear in a doughnut shape because the mid-region of the gas sphere is very thin compared with the relative thickness of its edges. MOUNT WILSON AND LAS CAMPANAS OBSERVATORIES

4▾

THE DAY THE SUN CAUGHT FIRE

A Big Bang Beginning

In the beginning there was the *Big Bang,* the explosion of a cosmic superatom that contained everything the Universe was to become. Just after the explosion nearly all of the Universe was a hot cloud of hydrogen. Over the next several seconds, some of the hydrogen fused into helium. Then over the next minute or so, the hydrogen spread out so thinly that no more fusions were possible. Only a few minutes after the Universe began, nine out of every ten atoms were hydrogen, the remaining one-tenth helium. That is the picture the Big Bang theory paints, and the more we learn about the Universe, the more evidence we find to support the theory. So until a better idea comes along, a Big Bang beginning seems reasonable.

We now move the cosmic clock ahead about a hundred thousand to a million years. The scene we find is one of great clouds of a mixture of hydrogen and helium, all rushing away from one another. Those clouds evolved into the billions of galaxies, but just how remains a major astronomical puzzle. So far as we can tell, all the galaxies seem to be between ten billion and fifteen billion years old, more than twice the age of the Sun. All that we observe going on in the night sky had been underway long before the Sun was born.

We can imagine the early galaxies containing billions of lumpy, local clouds of hydrogen and helium. The more massive and tightly packed clouds gravitationally attract and gobble up less massive ones and grow at their expense. For millions of years chaos rules, but order is in the making. It comes as the matter of the more massive clouds begins to organize into giant lopsided spheres, many the size of the entire Solar System, others much larger. Gravity is the organizer, packing and heating the spheres until they begin to shine faintly as new stars, called *protostars.* The sky is aglow with an array of the variables, dwarfs, and giants described in the previous chapter.

TURNING ON THE SUN

We move our cosmic clock ahead once more. The time is now some five billion years ago, and the place is out near the edge of the Milky Way. One of those great clouds of hydrogen and helium has, over millions of years, been collecting mass by gravitationally gobbling up surrounding gas clouds. And then an event that will shape the destiny of that cloud occurs. For eons a cloud of heavy elements— including carbon, silicon, iron, and many others—cast off by a supernova explosion has been racing across space on a collision course with our solar cloud of hydrogen and helium. Some of the elements forged by that supernova clump as compounds and form cosmic dust that mixes with and enriches our solar cloud. The cloud continues its gravitational collapse over millions more years.

As matter keeps tumbling in toward the cloud's center, the temperature and pressure rise until the central region begins to glow. At first it glows a cool dull red, then cherry red as it grows hotter. As matter continues to fall into that central core region, any slight rotation the cloud had becomes magnified by the conservation of angular momentum. So the cloud begins to spin faster. Finally, the rapid spinning causes the outer parts of the cloud to flatten out as a disk, like a pizza crust spun in the air. Within the dense disk matter silicates clump and form stony meteoroids and asteroids. Iron and nickel dust grains also clump and form metal meteoroids and asteroids. Astronomers now think that these lesser bodies formed some 4.55 billion years ago, ahead of the planets, for meteorites are the oldest bits of the Universe scientists have so far been able to date with certainty.

For about fifty million years this drama unfolds, until finally the temperature in the proto-Sun's core reaches about 12 million degrees. The crushing pressure and intense heat now combine and ignite the nuclear furnace that begins to roar and fuse hydrogen into helium. The protostar has become that star we call the Sun, shining with an intense yellowish white light.

PLANETS FORM

Imagine that we are poised high above the new Sun almost five billion years ago. We would see, as if through a fog, the top half of a brilliant central ball of violently churning gases. It is embedded in a broad spinning disk of cool gases and clumps of cosmic debris stretching away seemingly forever. The new Sun had by this time organized its matter for nuclear energy production. Meanwhile, the surrounding disk material was organizing itself into planets, moons, comets, ices, and asteroids. It was to take a hundred million years for the cosmic debris to collide and stick together as objects called *planetesimals*—rocks mixed with iron and other metals, and boulders the size of mountains. The sticking force was gravity.

As some planetesimals collided, they simply shattered and flew apart. Others were nudged into new orbits that flung them into the Sun. Still others were sent on courses outside the disk as cosmic exiles. The more massive clumps gravitationally swept up less massive ones and grew larger. If they were larger than about two hundred miles (320 kilometers) across, gravity pulled them into a sphere shape. If they were smaller, they remained irregular lumps, like the two moons of Mars and the asteroids Gaspra and Ida.

The Galileo space probe made this image of the asteroid 243 Ida from a distance of 2,175 miles (3,500 kilometers). Only the second asteroid to be approached by a space probe, Ida is a giant about 32 miles (52 kilometers) long. Many craters are visible. Ida is a stony fragment that most likely broke off a larger object during a collision. NASA

The larger sphere-shaped objects became the *protoplanets*. As each one acquired enough mass to withstand collisions by lesser planetesimals, it continued to be bombarded for millions of years. All the while it collected more mass. Astronomers think that at one stage a planetesimal a bit smaller than Mars crashed into Earth and splashed off matter that became the Moon. The young planets continued to be targets for planetesimals during their first 600 million years, but the deluge of rock and metal rains lessened some four billion years ago and has remained rare ever since. We have very convincing proof of such cosmic violence in the early Solar System. The Moon has thousands of impact craters. There are more than one hundred fifty impact craters still visible on Earth. And there are thousands more on Mercury, Mars, and the moons of the gas giant planets.

Most of the action seems to have been near the Sun, where the disk matter circled faster than farther out where Jupiter and the other gas giants formed. Violence reigned supreme in the region where the inner planets, Mercury, Venus, Earth, and Mars, took shape. Lower temperatures farther out in the disk permitted volatile materials such as methane and ammonia to solidify into planetesimals. There were more and larger planetesimals out in this region, and they built up into very large planets with cores of rock and metal.

The planet Mercury is one of the most heavily cratered objects in the solar system. All of the planets were pelted by millions of fragments of disk matter long after they were formed. Space debris continues to smash into the planets to this day, but much less often than when the Solar System was young.
NASA

Unlike the less massive inner planets, the more massive outer ones—Jupiter, Saturn, Uranus, and Neptune—attracted and held onto large amounts of disk gases. Among those gases were hydrogen, helium, methane, and ammonia. Such gases make up the bulk of the outer planets' atmospheres today, but they are not present in the atmospheres of the inner planets because of their higher temperatures and low surface gravity.

The planetesimals that orbited between Mars and Jupiter had an interesting fate: Jupiter's strong gravitation prevented them from collecting into a planet. To this day they swarm as billions of pieces of rock and metal called *asteroids* and *meteoroids*. Occasionally, these rogue members of the Solar System collide and speed off along new orbits that may send them crashing into Earth. One such errant missile

From time to time asteroid impacts on the Moon, Mars, and Venus splash off rock fragments that strike Earth as meteorites. This meteorite flung to Earth from Mars landed in Antarctica some 13,000 years ago. Some scientists suspected that the rock might contain evidence of primitive Martian life forms, but others disagreed. NASA

crashed into us sixty-five million years ago and probably spelled doom to dinosaurs and numerous other animals and plants. Scientists think they have found the crater formed by the asteroid in the seafloor off the coast of the Yucatán Peninsula.

On July 4, 1997 the robot Martian explorer Pathfinder *landed on the Red Planet. The mission sent back thousands of photographs before its radios went silent after four months. This image was taken on the third day and shows the small robot geologist named* Sojourner *examing Martian rocks.* NASA

At the outermost edge of the solar disk, there remained a spherical halo of ices that enclosed the Sun and its young family of planets in a frigid cocoon. This cloud of trillions of "dirty snowballs," as one astronomer has called them, is the Solar System's main store of comets. Whenever a passing star's gravity disturbs the icy cloud, it flings one or more comets in toward the Sun. A second, but lesser, store of comets called the Kuiper Belt lies closer to us, a bit beyond Pluto. In 1997, astronomers discovered one Kuiper Belt ice ball some three hundred miles (480 kilometers) across. Pluto may well be a giant Kuiper Belt object that escaped the belt and settled into an orbit about the Sun as an imposter planet. In 1996 astronomers discovered still another ice giant. Named 1996 TL66, it is about 310 miles (500 kilometers) in diameter and circles the Sun in a long, stretched-out orbit that takes it far beyond distant Pluto, out to a distance 130 times greater than Earth's distance from the Sun. There may be many other such giant icebergs out there in the no-man's-land of the Solar System, all left-over matter of the original solar disk that escaped capture by the gas giant planets when they were forming.

After the planets had formed, the Solar System was still a dusty and dim place. However, during the eons in which the Sun's nuclear reactor was firing up, the Sun gave off violent bursts of energy. The resulting solar gales of atomic debris swept the space between the planets nearly clean of the remaining fog of gas and dust grains. However, to this day a thin veil of dust remains, and we see it as the dimly shining *zodiacal light.*

Astronomers have at least four reasons for thinking that the planets formed right along with the Sun by gravitationally sweeping up matter from the solar disk. 1) All the planets orbit the Sun pretty much as if on the surface of a cosmic racetrack, although Mercury and Pluto break the rule slightly by having somewhat tilted orbits. And considering that Pluto may be a captured Kuiper Belt object, we can discount it. 2) The racetrack plane along which the planets move, stretching out from the Sun's equator, strongly suggests that the planets formed out of the Sun's solar disk matter. 3) If you could look down on the Solar System from above Earth's North Pole, you would see all the planets moving about the Sun in the same direction, counterclockwise. That is the same direction as the Sun's rotation on its axis. 4) The orbits of the planets, except for Mercury and Pluto, are nearly circular. Such orderly movements are convincing evidence that the planets' parent solar disk matter was in orderly motion about a rotating Sun.

The violent activity of solar disk matter in the early Solar System has long been replaced by a beautifully stable Sun and system of planets ordered by the laws of motion and gravitation. We now think that planets more often than not form right along with stars, and that we, along with planet Earth, are made up of the chemical elements of the original solar disk cloud. We, too, are by-products of the Sun's formation. Atoms that long ago were exploded out of a distant, dying star and mixed with the gases of our solar cloud some five billion years ago are now the matter of our very bodies.

It is time that we sharpen our focus on Earth—that ball of rock and metal adorned with life, bathed with water, and protected within a soft cocoon of air—and find out how it has fared over the ages under a Sun that has gradually become larger and brighter, as it continues to do today.

5.

EARTH LIFE: A SOLAR CONNECTION

EARTH'S HOT BEGINNING

The violent sweep-up process of planetesimals that formed Earth heated the young planet to some 3,600°F (2,000°C). The materials it collected included hydrogen, helium, carbon, nitrogen, oxygen, iron, aluminum, gold, uranium, sulfur, phosphorus, and silicon. The radioactive elements uranium, thorium, and potassium also played a role in heating the planet from within. Perhaps half a billion years after the planet formed, it was a soupy globe of molten rock and metal, but as the planetesimal bombardment eased, probably between 4.2 and 4.4 billion years ago, Earth slowly cooled. Meanwhile, the heavier materials, such as iron and nickel, sank and formed Earth's core region. The lighter silicates floated to the surface and became crustal rock. Meanwhile, thousands of tons of fine dust containing carbon compounds continued to rain down on the young planet, perhaps ten thousand or more tons a year, but it was not enough to produce further heating. To this day some three hundred tons of cosmic dust and other debris are swept up by Earth each year.

As the planet cooled, many gases bubbled out of solution and began to form an atmosphere. The gases included hydrogen, water vapor, nitrogen, carbon monoxide, and carbon dioxide, along with smaller amounts of methane, ammonia, and hydrogen sulfide. But there was little oxygen at this stage. As water vapor continued to collect from outgassing and comets, it condensed and fell as rain. For perhaps a hundred thousand years it rained, and the water collected in pools that formed shallow, warm seas.

A discovery made in the mid-1980s suggested that much of Earth's vast water supply could have come from space in the form of small comets about the size of a house. Researchers in 1997 claim to have spotted evidence of such a rain of comet ice balls, some 40,000 a day, raining down on Earth at the rate of five to thirty a minute. We never see the comets, the researchers say, because they are torn apart and changed into clouds of water vapor at distances from hundreds to thousands of miles. The clouds are then attracted into the atmosphere and eventually condense and fall as rain. Atmospheric scientists estimate that this process of comet rain has been going for millions of years, adding an inch or so (two-and-a-half centimeters) of water every 20,000 years. Over Earth's long history, such a collection of comet water could add up to an ocean or two. Interestingly, the comet water also contains a rich array of carbon compounds, molecules of a kind that could have nurtured the origin of life on our planet. In 1998 astronomers took a hard look at this once-promising idea. Many doubt that such a current rain of comet water is taking place today, although it most likely did occur during Earth's early life.

FROM CHEMICALS TO "LIVING" MATTER

A recipe for life: The right mixture of chemicals from a cosmic cloud, add sunlight, then stir for about half a billion years.

For life as we know it to have started on Earth, the planet must have had at least twenty special chemicals. The elements hydrogen, carbon, nitrogen, oxygen, phosphorus, and sulfur make up about ninety-five percent of most animals and plants. Other elements needed in lesser amounts include potassium, sodium, magnesium, calcium, and chlorine.

So far as we can tell, life arose in the early warm seas. Chemists have shown that energy from the Sun, from lightning, and from other sources can cause carbon, oxygen, nitrogen, and hydrogen to bond and form the complex molecules needed for life. Among these molecules are certain chemical building blocks called *amino acids.* They combine with each other to form those still larger building blocks of living matter known as proteins. Plants and animals alike use proteins for growth, for the repair of injured parts, and as a source of energy.

In recent years, astronomers have discovered that certain life-giving chemicals exist in space and in meteorites and comets. It now seems possible that some key molecules necessary for life arrived here in comets and meteorites early in our planet's history. Among such imported giant molecules found in meteorites are several different kinds of amino acids.

At the same time, over the past several years oceanographers have discovered complex communities of organisms living around undersea geysers that spew out clouds of hot water rich in many minerals. The minerals build up yellow, orange, green, and white cones, depending on the minerals doing the building. The cones form when sea water seeps deeply into cracks in the seafloor, is heated, and comes bubbling back out again. From depths of many miles the heated water dissolves many minerals and carries them up to the seafloor. Some cones contain mostly iron, others are rich in copper, and still others silver or zinc.

While most of the deep-sea floor is a vast desert with hardly any life, the fifteen or more undersea geysers so far discovered support a wondrous diversity of organisms. Hundreds of new species have been found. There are foot-long clams, eyeless shrimp, and giant tube worms. These plant-animal communities survive entirely on energy and nutrients from Earth's deep interior, not on energy from sunlight. The basic nutrient is hydrogen sulfide, which is poisonous to most life but which certain bacteria thrive on. Those bacteria then feed organisms higher up the food chain, such as clams and mussels. So rich and self-sufficient are these seafloor geyser communities that some biologists wonder if the first life on Earth might have originated on the deep-sea floor, energized not by the Sun, but by the terrible heat and pressure of the inferno of molten rock deep within the planet. Such conditions favorable for the origin of life on the seafloor surely were even more common early in Earth's history than today.

But how could nonliving molecules, no matter how complex, and no matter whether from space or from the bowels of the planet, become living matter? Here we may be setting a word trap for ourselves by thinking of certain things as living and others as not living, with nothing in between. We might think instead of an unbroken chain of chemical forms ranging from elements to simple molecules to complex clumps of molecules, and eventually to systems of molecules that resemble the matter that we say is "living." If, indeed, life developed in this manner, the process must have taken perhaps half a billion years.

The next stage in the evolution of living matter might have been complex groupings of large molecules into microscopic units enclosed within protective jackets, or membranes. Such clumps of living matter were early forms of protein. From what we can observe about living matter today, we can imagine those early proteinlike units "feeding" on certain complex food molecules by sucking them in through tiny openings in their protective membranes. We can also imagine some of these proteinlike clumps becoming clever in a way that gave them an advantage. Instead of taking in existing food molecules, they took in other, smaller molecules and then assembled them into food. Since there would be more of the smaller molecules in the outside environment than ready-made food molecules, those protein-like clumps able to make their own food would have an advantage over those that had to find their food ready-made in some Precambrian Burger King. So instead of depending on the nearest fast food shop, they bought flour and other ingredients and made their own food.

In some such process, the first living cells evolved. Cells are the smallest organized units of living matter recognized by biologists. And those early cells became expert at making their own food out of raw materials in the outside environment. The raw materials were molecules of carbon dioxide and water vapor. With sunlight as a source of energy, the cells combined the carbon dioxide and water and made a sugar called glucose. In the process they gave off oxygen as "waste" matter. These are the organisms that might have evolved as early as some 3.7 or 3.9 billion years ago.

Do we have evidence of such early organisms? Yes. The fossils of thirty kinds of microscopic plants found in Bitter Springs, Australia are 900 million years old. Fourteen of them are like certain green plants—algae—living today. Microscopic algae from 1.6 to 2.0 billion years old have been found in rock along the shore of Lake Superior in Ontario, as have rod-shaped bacteria. Still older fossils of microscopic bacteria-like organisms 3.1 billion years old have been found near Fig Tree, South Africa. They are similar to blue-green algae living today. Even older microscopic organisms like those found near Fig Tree have been found in Swaziland, Africa. They are from 3.4 to

3.6 or more billion years old. There is no doubt that life established itself very early in Earth's history.

At first the oxygen freed by those primitive plants was quickly absorbed by iron and other oxygen-hungry elements on the land and in the early seas. Eventually, however, the seas' appetite for oxygen was satisfied, and free oxygen began to build up in the atmosphere. Eventually, the oxygen content of the air grew to twenty-one percent, the level at which it remains today. But to remain at that level requires a steady output of new oxygen from blue-green algae in the seas and from the planet's vast regions of grasslands and forests. If oxygen production by plants seriously decreased, the free oxygen in the air would be consumed as it combined with other elements on Earth's surface—with lava produced by volcanoes, for example.

There are many gaps in our knowledge of the chain of chemical events that led to the first cells. Even so, most biologists agree that some such broad outline seems likely. Biologists also generally agree that with the right conditions—the right blend of matter and energy—life of some sort is bound to arise due to natural causes. This must be the rule not only on Earth, but elsewhere in the Universe as well. Although we do not have firm evidence of life elsewhere in the Universe, the chances that it does exist seem overwhelming.

6▾
TIME AND CHANGE

CLIMATES OF YESTERYEAR

The fossil record goes back more than 3.5 billion years. By studying fossils recovered the world over, scientists called *paleoclimatologists* are able to reconstruct past climates. In general, there are two major types of climate—warm and glacial. We are now living in a glacial period, or more correctly at the tail end of an interglacial period. Glacial periods have not been the rule throughout Earth's long history. Warm periods have been much more common. During the warmest of the warm periods, ice was probably unknown anywhere on the planet. About a hundred million years ago, when dinosaurs thundered over the land, Earth's climate was some 27°F (15°C) warmer than now, and there were no polar ice caps.

Then some 60 million years ago, near the beginning of the Tertiary Period, things began to cool, and they have been cool ever since. Over the past 700,000 years seven ice ages have come and gone. Ninety percent of that period was colder than it is now. Ice is still the rule today and will be for a while. The glacial cycles work something like this: Each cycle of peak glacial activity—from one peak, through an interglacial period, then to the peak of the next glacial period—lasts about 100,000 years. From the end of one glacial period to the beginning of the next lasts about 10,000 years.

We entered our present *interglacial* period of warming some 13,000 years ago, at which time the climate became wetter, and the world temperature rose some 8°F (5°C). The glacial peak came about 18,000 years ago. At that time ice covered 20 million square miles (52 million square kilometers) of Earth's surface and formed on both the Northern and Southern Hemispheres. That amounts to about thirty percent of the planet's total land surface. The average thickness of the ice was 4,000 feet (1,200 meters). During an ice age sea level may drop by 475 feet (145 meters) because such a large amount of water is locked up as ice. But then during the following

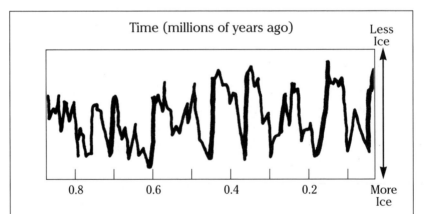

Over the past 700,000 years there have been seven known ice ages, after which a period of warming (heavy lines) occurred. The most recent period of warming (heavy line at far right) has brought us to a stage where it is now warmer than it has been for more than ninety percent of the past million years. AFTER NATIONAL RESEARCH COUNCIL

interglacial period, sea level rises as the ice melts. It may rise as much as 260 feet (80 meters) higher than it is today. At the height of the last glacial period, you could have walked from England to France, from Alaska across to Siberia, and from New Guinea to Australia.

USING OXYGEN TO READ PAST CLIMATES

How do paleoclimatologists manage to read Earth's climate history? They use "fossil" oxygen as a thermometer to read the temperatures of ancient seas and the atmosphere. Most of the oxygen of the air and that dissolved in lakes, rivers, and oceans has an atomic weight of 16 and is written ^{16}O. But there is a heavier form of oxygen, ^{18}O, called an *isotope.* One interesting thing about these two forms of oxygen is that the ratio of one to the other changes with the temperature of the water. For example, ocean water at 50°F (10°C) has a higher ratio of ^{18}O to ^{16}O than ocean water at 86°F (30°C). When water evaporates from the sea as water vapor, condensing out first as clouds and then falling as rain or snow, more of the lighter-weight ^{16}O enters the air than does the heavier-weight ^{18}O. So we would expect a bucket of snow or a cloud to contain a higher 16 to 18 ratio than a bucket of warmer sea water.

Fossil shells of tiny marine animals called *foraminifera,* which lived many millions of years ago, have been preserved in the ocean-bottom sediments. To this day they still contain oxygen that they took in from sea water. By measuring the ^{18}O to ^{16}O ratio, chemists can read the water temperatures when the foraminifera were alive. For example, measurements show that 32 million years ago Antarctica's ocean water was as warm as that now off the coast of Rhode Island. Waters of the Arctic were similarly warm at that time. Further evidence for that warm Antarctic climate comes from fossils that show that parts of Greenland that are now without trees were then sprawling forests of pine and spruce.

The oxygen isotope thermometer can also be used to measure the temperature of the air many thousands of years ago. Glaciers are formed by a gradual accumulation of snow that becomes packed as ice. Since the air from which polar snows form is warmer in summer than in winter, we would expect the glacial ice formed from the packed snow to occur in summer-winter layers. And they do. When climatologists drill a deep core of ice from a glacier, they have a record of air temperatures going back to the time the ice was formed layer by layer. Ice cores taken in Antarctica and Greenland, extending down more than a thousand feet (305 meters), give us an unbroken temperature profile of the past 10,000 to 100,000 years.

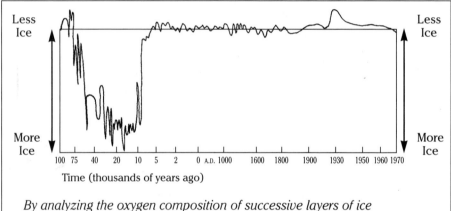

By analyzing the oxygen composition of successive layers of ice collected by a glacier over many centuries, climatologists can tell cold from warm periods. Greenland ice cores reveal a temperature record over the past 100,000 years. (The curve is squeezed at the left because the large time span is given less horizontal space.) AFTER W. DANSGAARD

WHAT CAUSES CLIMATE CHANGE?

Only over the last twenty years or so have climatologists come to an agreement about what triggers climate change. In general, two major groups of causes have been talked about—geographical causes and astronomical causes. Among geographical causes cited have been the wandering about of the continents due to plate movement, the accompanying change in the location and circulation of seas, changes in elevation of the land due to mountain building, large-scale volcano outpourings, and changes in circulation and composition of the atmosphere.

One or more geographical causes acting together or separately can certainly bring on short-term climate change and have many times in the past. For example, the impact of a large asteroid or comet would be catastrophic and fill the air with tremendous amounts of dust and other debris. The debris would be caught up in the global air circulation and stay there for years. As a result, a significant amount of heat and light from the Sun would never reach Earth's surface. Just such an asteroid impact some 65 million years ago is now believed to have helped send the dinosaurs on

During the most recent ice age, which peaked about 18,000 years ago, ice covered about thirty percent of Earth's total land surface (white areas) in both hemispheres. Antarctica is not shown.

Today   18,000 years ago

their way to extinction, along with millions of other plant and animal species.

In 1815 a volcano known as Mount Tambora, in Indonesia, erupted and cast an estimated 36 cubic miles (150 cubic kilometers) of ash into the atmosphere. Clouds of the airborne ash were so thick that an area extending 300 miles (480 kilometers) from the volcano was in darkness for three days. In the United States and Europe, the next year was called "the year without a summer." Temperatures dropped by amounts ranging from 1.8°F (1°C) to 5.5°F (3°C). In some places it rained every day—except for three or four days—from May to October. In New England it snowed in June. In 1816 there were frosts every month of the year.

Although climatologists are interested in geographical events that may bring short-term climate change, they also want to know what changes climate over the long haul of millions of years. And that brings us to the likelihood of astronomical causes for climate change, specifically the Sun-Earth relationship

Just before the year 1900, the English astronomer E. Walter Maunder made a discovery that raised the eyebrows of other astronomers. A search through old books and journals convinced him that from about 1645 to 1715 sunspots had all but vanished from the Sun along with certain other solar activity, such as the solar flares that cause the colorful auroras high in Earth's atmosphere near the poles. Just a few years before this period, however, when Galileo was observing the Sun, sunspots had been in evidence. Between the years 1100 and 1250, naked-eye observations of the Sun indicate that sunspots were plentiful. (Looking directly at the Sun can seriously harm the eyes, as Galileo discovered.) They occurred right along with a period of warming that enabled the Vikings to explore Greenland and sail to the New World. Sunspots were observed again later in the 1700s. Maunder concluded that during a single year the "normal" Sun generates more sunspots than were seen during that entire seventy-year period ending in 1715. The period has come to be known as the *Maunder sunspot minimum.*

Since Maunder's time, evidence has become very convincing that periods of high solar activity and low solar activity tend to influence short-term climate change over periods lasting between fifty and several hundred years. But what about longer periods? What astronomical events involving the Sun-Earth relationship might bring on an ice age, or bring one to an end?

EARTH'S ORBITAL DANCES

Long-term climate change depends on how Earth manages to distribute the greater or lesser amounts of energy it receives from the Sun from time to time. Earth dances to several tunes as it revolves about the Sun, and all are orchestrated by the mysterious force of gravity.

As Earth orbits the Sun, its attitude in space changes in three ways that cause periodic climate change. In 1842, the French mathematician Joseph Alphonse Adhémar said that the ice ages probably come and go because of Earth's erratic orbital dance. Then twenty years later, another investigator explained how Earth's long-term change in distance from the Sun might change climate. In the 1930s and 1940s, the Yugoslavian geophysicist Milutin Milankovitch fine-tuned the idea by adding Earth's wobble and tilt to the picture. So the astronomical group of possible climate-change causes offers three major Earth rhythms, sometimes called the *Milankovitch cycles.* Here's how they work, starting with the shortest cycle.

Precession is one way in which Earth's attitude in space changes. Tilted over at its present angle of 23.5°, Earth wobbles like a slowly spinning top about to fall over. It completes one wobble-cycle about every 25,800 years. Today, our Northern Hemisphere winter occurs when Earth is at its closest to the Sun, in January. But 10,500 years ago precession had our Northern Hemisphere winter occurring when Earth was most distant from the Sun, at the opposite side of its orbit. Theoretically, winters in the Northern Hemisphere then should have been colder than they are now, and summers hotter. So precession is what decides whether summer, for example, is going to be hotter than "usual," or cooler.

When the Northern Hemisphere of the planet is tilted back away from the Sun at a time when Earth is most distant from the Sun, Earth is in precessional winter. At such times the lesser amount of sunlight striking the Northern Hemisphere causes more snow to accumulate in winter and less snow to melt in summer. The result is increased glacial activity and a build up of the polar ice caps.

The second-longest cycle is the slow change in the amount our planet is tilted on its axis. Today it is tilted, or inclined, 23.5° with respect to the plane of its orbit about the Sun. We call this tilt its *obliquity,* and it is Earth's obliquity that causes our changing seasons. It is not the planet's changing distance from the sun in the course of a year, as many people believe. Earth's range of change in obliquity has been estimated at between 21.5° and 24.5°. The greater the tilt, the greater the seasonal contrast at a given time. The less the tilt, the less seasonal difference there will be. The change in obliquity from least to greatest and back again occurs in cycles of about 41,000 years.

The third and longest orbital dance cycle Earth goes through is its varying mean distance from the Sun, called its *eccentricity.* Eccentricity varies from zero to a value of about 0.06 once about every 100,000 years. When at its greatest eccentricity and farthest distance from the Sun, Earth receives about twenty percent less solar radiation than when it is closest to the Sun. This is a significant amount when you consider that a drop of only thirteen percent would bring on a super ice age, covering Earth's entire surface with a blanket of ice one mile (1.6 kilometers) thick. A rise of thirty percent would bring on a heat wave that would destroy virtually all Earth life. The reason Earth's orbit gets stretched out somewhat and then

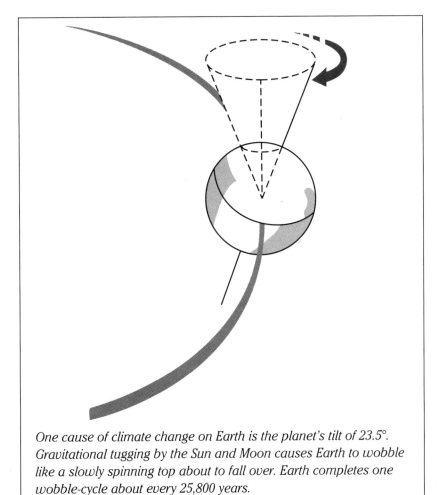

*One cause of climate change on Earth is the planet's tilt of 23.5°.
Gravitational tugging by the Sun and Moon causes Earth to wobble
like a slowly spinning top about to fall over. Earth completes one
wobble-cycle about every 25,800 years.*

later compressed to a more circular shape is that it is affected by the
gravitational tug of the other planets.

Now what sense can we make out of the three cycles as they
might apply to Earth's long-term climate change? In the 1970s, scientists doing a study called project Climap analyzed the oxygen isotope
ratios of hundreds of ocean-bottom cores taken from the Southern

Hemisphere. They concluded that the changes in Earth's orbit just described have contributed to the advance and retreat of ice over the past two million years. Their seafloor cores contained oxygen isotope climate records over the past 450,000 years. They found peaks of climate change occurring roughly every 23,000 years, which comes close to the 25,800-year cycle of precessional wobbling. Another series of climatic peaking was found to occur every 42,000 years, which nicely fits the 41,000-year cycle of obliquity shifting. And a third series of climatic peaks occurs about every 100,000 years, which fits the cycle of eccentricity change. Those are the kinds of numbers that warm an investigator's heart.

Even so, it would be misleading to say that the puzzle of Earth's long-term climate change has been solved. It hasn't, even though at least a little bit of the mystery has been removed. Although ice ages come and go every hundred thousand years, at least in recent geologic time, climatologists doubt that the stretching of Earth's orbit alone has been responsible for the rhythm. Other influences must be at work also. But what influences? Recall that the Sun is a variable star and not an absolutely reliable radiator of the same amount of energy year by year and century by century.

Climate is shaped and reshaped by a combination of the Sun's energy output with the interaction of land movements, changes in the oceans, and the air. When enormous land masses, such as the Tibetan Plateau and the Himalayas, are thrust up, there is an accompanying shift in wind, weather, and ocean circulation patterns. Possibly such monumental land mass changes set the geological mood for the ages of ice that began near the beginning of the Tertiary Period about 50 million years ago, and then the orbital dances of Earth pushed the change along.

Another contributing cause was probably the migration of the Antarctica continent from its once tropical paradise near the Equator to the frigid bottom of the planet.

No, there are too many pieces to the climate puzzle. Although we think we have identified most of them, we're not quite sure how they all fit together. For example, there is the carbon dioxide piece of the puzzle. Over the past 160,000 years temperatures have gone up whenever the carbon dioxide level has gone up. During an inter-glacial period the air contains about a third more carbon dioxide than ice-age air does. Why? Today our factories and automobiles fill the air with more carbon dioxide than those past 160,000 years had ever seen. While it seems certain that pumping more and more car-bon dioxide into the air is bound to cause short-term warming, we cannot say what the long-term effects may be. The orbital dances of Earth may simply override the effects and bring on a new era of cold no matter what we do. Does a natural increase in the carbon dioxide content of the air somehow follow an ice age or precede it? We don't know. And what about those glacial mini–periods that last a few decades to a century or so? Are they triggered by short-term changes in the energy output of the Sun, the effects of a flickering Sun resem-bling the flickering of an old fluorescent light tube before it burns out? The Maunder sunspot minimum suggests that from time to time our solar power plant can indeed trigger such short-term changes in global climate.

Solar astronomer John A. Eddy is convinced that "the present-day frequency of sunspots and auroras is probably unusual, and that since the 1600s the activity of the Sun has risen steadily to a very high level—a level perhaps unequaled [over the past million years]."

Eddy further reports that examination of bristlecone pine annual growth rings gives us a measure of the change in solar activity going back some 7,000 years. He has shown that over most of that period mountain glaciers have come and gone in pace with increases and decreases in solar activity. "Every rise in solar activity . . . matches a time of glacier retreat," he reported. He concludes: "These early results in comparing solar history with climate make it appear that changes on the Sun are the dominant agent of climate changes lasting between 50 and several hundred years."

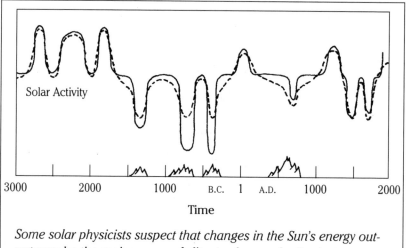

Some solar physicists suspect that changes in the Sun's energy output may be the major cause of climate changes lasting between fifty and several hundred years. The solid line in the diagram represents solar activity over the past five thousand years, based on the abundance of carbon-14 in the growth rings of bristlecone pine trees. The broken line represents solar activity based on a possible sunspot cycle. The four glacial mountains along the bottom line represent times when Alpine glaciers advanced. AFTER J. EDDY

THE WEAK-YOUNG-SUN PARADOX

A paradox is any idea that appears to contradict itself. And the notion that the Sun pours out thirty percent more energy today than it did in its youth, but has not burned Earth to a crisp, does just that.

The Sun is growing brighter and brighter and hotter and hotter because of the growing store of helium in its core. It keeps making helium as it burns hydrogen during energy production. The buildup of the heavier helium makes the core denser. A denser core speeds hydrogen fusions, which turns up the heat and makes the Sun shine more fiercely. Surprisingly, fossil evidence shows that Earth's overall climate has not grown steadily hotter throughout geologic time, as we might expect from a hotter-burning Sun. In fact, it is even cooler today than it was a hundred million years ago, and ice ages have come and gone several times.

We must ask what prevented Earth long ago from developing a killer climate all the time the Sun was growing hotter. Also, because the young Sun put out only about seventy percent as much energy as it radiates today, conditions some 3.5 billion years ago should have been cold, so cold that the new oceans should have frozen. But they didn't. Fossil evidence tells us that life was abundant in warm seas during those early years. A cooler Sun at that time should have discouraged the complex chemistry that got life started. And a thirty percent brighter Sun today is a VERY much brighter star and should have done us all in by now. That is the paradox. Something managed to keep early Earth warm when the Sun was cool, and today keeps us cool as the Sun keeps getting hotter.

Our planet's remarkable thermostat that controls heat at Earth's surface is the atmosphere, whose global circulation is driven by the Sun. It seems to work something like this:

When the planet was young it must have had a lot of carbon dioxide in its atmosphere, possibly a thousand times more than today. The high carbon dioxide content of Venus's atmosphere today acts as a blanket that traps heat and keeps the planet's surface at a deadly 900°F (480°C). A block of lead placed on Venus's surface would just melt and flow away. That greenhouse effect of carbon dioxide in young Earth's atmosphere is probably what kept the planet warm when the Sun was cooler.

As the Sun kept growing hotter, Earth's oceans, rocks, and atmosphere acted to decrease the carbon dioxide content of the air.

Initially the planet heated up just enough to evaporate large enough amounts of ocean water and cause heavy rainfalls. Rain removes carbon dioxide from the air. The result has been a less and less effective greenhouse heat trap, allowing the planet to radiate its "excess" heat off into space. Over geologic time, the cooling process seems to have worked well and the atmosphere's natural carbon dioxide content kept relatively low. But human activity has poured more and more carbon dioxide into the air, and with what results we cannot yet say for certain.

When rain absorbs carbon dioxide from the air, the weak acid carbonic acid is formed. It is carbonic acid that dissolves the noses and other sharp features of stone statues and monuments and blurs the writing on grave stones. As the ocean water absorbs carbon dioxide, many different kinds of marine organisms use the carbon dioxide to make their calcium carbonate shells. When those organisms die, they drift to the seafloor and become part of the carpet of sediments that are continually laid down. Over time the sediments are compressed into sedimentary rock, such as limestone and dolomite. The rock may then be thrust up as mountains that contain a rich store of carbon dioxide. In fact, Earth's rocks probably contain as much stored carbon dioxide as there is in Venus's atmosphere, which is ninety-six percent carbon dioxide.

Raising the air's carbon dioxide content, as industrial activity is doing rapidly today, may produce an interesting side effect—that of increasing the amount of water vapor in the air. An increased amount of water vapor would trap more heat radiation from Earth's surface and so tend to add to global warming. But there is a second side effect—increased cloud cover due to the increased amount of water vapor. Just a 2.4 percent increase in the amount of cloud cover could lower the average surface temperature by about 2°C and so cancel out the greenhouse effect! Again, there are so many interacting pieces to the climate puzzle that it is difficult to know how to fit them all together. Generally, it all amounts to a continuing Sun-Earth relationship, a relationship in which both the Sun and Earth, as dynamic cosmic bodies, are evolving.

Two things are certain. First, there is an interplay between Earth's living matter and the air, oceans, and land. Second, even though the Sun has grown hotter over the past four billion years or so, Earth life from the earliest times has somehow held on. Once started, it has stubbornly survived numerous environmental catastrophes, refusing to be snuffed out. This continued success of the planet's living matter has led two scientists to speculate that Earth life has somehow developed the ability to control the environment, to keep it comfortable for its survival. Species come and go with environmental change, but life itself goes on. This idea is called the *Gaia hypothesis* and was developed by the British scientist James Lovelock and the American biologist Lynn Margulis.

Earth life seems to be safe for a while. Still, it is only a matter of time before the Sun puts on the last show and ends that marvel of creation it spawned a few billion years ago. But before playing out that last scene, let's consider something called "habitable life zones" for a planetary system. We will then be in a much better position to appreciate Earth's final moments as a planet, and the Sun's final moments as a star.

7.

PLANETS FOR LIFE

Twenty years ago I wrote a book with the title *Beyond Earth: The Search for Extraterrestrial Life.* On rereading the book for possible ideas to include in this chapter, I have been impressed by two things: first, how little our ideas and expectations for life on other worlds have changed over those years; and second, how impressive advances in technology have been, advances that will one day soon enable us to detect Earthlike planets many light-years away and at the same time analyze their atmospheres for signs of life. But before looking at that exciting new technology, let's examine the conditions a planet, and its local star, must be able to offer in order for intelligent life to evolve, develop a civilization, and build the technology to maintain it.

HABITABLE ZONES FOR HABITABLE PLANETS

To be habitable by life forms high or low, a planet must lie within a certain range of distance from its local star. We will call that distance range the *habitable zone.* If the planet is too close, it will be too hot for the complex molecules needed for life either to form or to remain stable. We are assuming that the planet has such molecules, a liquid medium for them, and that the basic building blocks for the molecules are carbon. There is a lot of carbon out there in space, and no other known element has the talent for building such a large variety of molecules needed for life, at least for the kind of life we know. If the planet is too distant, it will be too cold for chemical reactions to proceed rapidly enough to build complex aggregates of molecules in the first place. Distance, of course, depends on the kind of star we imagine. For a large, hot star twenty-five times brighter than the Sun, an Earthlike planet would have to orbit at Jupiter's distance from the Sun to remain both cool and warm enough. For a red dwarf star only a tenth as bright as the Sun, an Earthlike planet would have to be much closer, about Mercury's distance from the Sun.

Just as important as the distance from its local star is the planet's mass. Mass influences several things—the planet's density, the strength of its gravitational attraction, its ability or inability to hold onto an ocean or an atmosphere, and the composition of that atmosphere, for example. So we should not hold out hopes for finding civilizations on planets much more massive or less massive than Earth. Stephen H. Dole, a researcher who has given much thought to the notion of habitable planets, suggests that the mass range of habitability lies between 0.4 times Earth's mass at the lower extreme and 2.35 times at the upper. That would mean a diameter of 6,180 miles (9,945 kilometers) for the smaller planet. The more massive planet with 2.35 Earth masses would have a diameter of 9,900 miles (15,932 kilometers), assuming Earth's average density. Earth's diameter is about 7,900 miles (12,700 kilometers).

The rate at which a planet rotates is also important to its potential habitability. For instance, the rate of rotation affects the daily temperature patterns, atmospheric circulation, and day length. A slowly rotating planet will tend to heat up more on its lighted side and cool off more on its shadow side than a more rapidly rotating planet, simply because it's sitting there in the light and shade longer than a more rapidly rotating planet. Dole estimates that an acceptable range of rotation might be from about a three-hour day for a fast planet to a ninety-six hour day for a slow planet.

Another thing we have to consider is the tilt of the planet's polar axis with respect to the plane of its orbit. If there is no tilt, then the length of day and night is equal throughout the year. Zero tilt would also mean no seasons, provided the planet's orbit were nearly circular. We have seasons on Earth because Earth's axis is tilted $23.5°$ with respect to the plane of its orbit.

At the opposite extreme from a planet with $0°$ tilt is one tipped over at an angle of $90°$, so that each of its poles is pointed directly at its local star during one complete phase of its revolution. In such a case one pole would be baked by direct sunlight for several months while the opposite pole would be freezing in shadow. A quarter of a year later the equatorial region would be heated most while both poles would be weakly illuminated. This would be a time of equal days and nights on the planet. Another quarter of a year later the previously frigid pole would be pointing directly at the planet's local star. And at the last quarter of the year direct equatorial heating would again be the rule.

Inhabitants living near the equatorial regions of such a planet would experience two "normal" warm seasons each year interrupted by two cold seasons. During both cold seasons, for days at a time their local star would hover near the horizon. Dole suggests that a planet with an equatorial tilt of more than about $80°$ would present extremely harsh environmental conditions capable of preventing an advanced civilization from developing.

Still another thing we have to consider is the kind of star a habitable planet revolves about. As you found earlier, there are

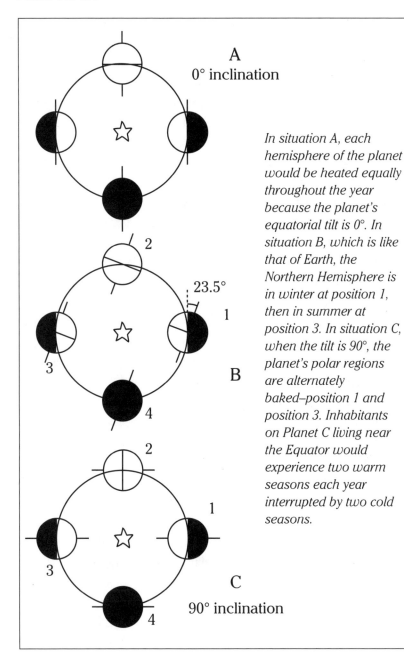

A
0° inclination

B

23.5°

C
90° inclination

In situation A, each hemisphere of the planet would be heated equally throughout the year because the planet's equatorial tilt is 0°. In situation B, which is like that of Earth, the Northern Hemisphere is in winter at position 1, then in summer at position 3. In situation C, when the tilt is 90°, the planet's polar regions are alternately baked–position 1 and position 3. Inhabitants on Planet C living near the Equator would experience two warm seasons each year interrupted by two cold seasons.

many kinds of stars. At one extreme are the blue supergiants, extremely hot stars with life-spans measured only in a few tens of millions of years or more. At the other extreme are the red dwarf stars, feeble radiators of energy with life-spans of a trillion years or so. Midway between are Sunlike stars, which are moderate radiators of energy with life-spans around 10 billion years. For reasons you will see in a moment, if a star has a short life-span, we can rule it out as supporting a technological civilization. We can likewise rule out stars that do not emit energy at a more or less constant rate for at least several billion years, stars such as red giants, white dwarfs, novae, supernovae, and variable stars whose energy output varies by a large amount.

About half the stars visible to us are members of double star systems, or clusters of three, four, or more stars all orbiting in gravitational association. Could we expect to find technological civilizations on planets revolving about such multiple-star systems? Before answering that question, we must ask two others. 1) Are the stars forming a double star system, for example, at such a distance from each other that the planets of each are able to maintain stable orbits and so avoid overheating and overcooling? 2) Is the total amount of radiation received by a planet, from both stars combined, constant enough and of the right intensity to permit biochemical and biological activity?

There are several interesting possibilities. For instance, imagine a double star system whose two stars are separated by a distance large enough to permit the planets of each star to maintain stable orbits and to maintain a temperature range that is tolerable. If the two stars were about two billion miles (3.2 billion kilometers) apart—about Uranus's distance from the Sun—then the more massive of the two stars could support planets out to a distance of about 640 million miles (one billion kilometers). Those planets would have both a stable orbit and a tolerable temperature range. The less massive of the two stars could also support habitable planets out to a distance of about 220 million miles (355 million kilometers).

Now imagine a double star system whose two stars are rather close to each other, millions instead of billions of miles. Planets revolving about either of these two stars would have highly unstable orbits and, as a result, temperature extremes that would discourage advanced biology. But we can also imagine one or more planets far enough removed from the closely associated star pair so that they orbit both stars and so have a double Sun. So the distance separating the members of a double-star system is important when we ask if such stars can support habitable planets. Since about fifty percent of all stars are double star systems, this consideration takes on added meaning.

Star Age as a Requirement

If we use Earth as our example—and we must since it's the only example we have—a technological civilization does not just appear overnight. Ours has had a long journey along the evolutionary trail that began with the origin of Earth life more than 3.5 billion years ago. If you want to push the "beginning" back to the time the Sun and planets formed, then the figure changes to some 4.6 billion years. So, reaching our present age of computers has required an enormous amount of time. Over that time the first living cells evolved into more complex life-forms, thus establishing a chain of life. Once started, that chain has not once been broken, and its myriad evolutionary pathways stagger the imagination.

In our attempts to find life elsewhere in the Universe we can narrow the search by ruling out not only erratic stars but all stars with short life-spans, those measured only in tens or hundreds of millions of years. We will make better use of our time by searching among Sunlike stars and the red dwarfs with their long life-spans. After all, we know that Earth sits comfortably within a habitable zone for life, so it will be wise to select as our primary targets for planetary investigation stars that most closely resemble our own Sun. Probably it will be just such stars that nurture and stir a chemical soup over a long enough period of time to set the wheels of organic evolution turning. The most momentous discovery in history would be to find such a planet where evolution has taken hold, stubbornly overcoming myriad false starts, dead ends, temporary setbacks, and has produced an alien equivalent of Picasso or Einstein, or Mozart, or the builders of the pyramids of Egypt.

Astronomers and physicists have abundant evidence that the laws of physics and chemistry that operate here on Earth also operate out there in the far reaches of the Galaxy and beyond. The universal law of gravitation works throughout the Universe—gently tugging the Pathfinder explorer to the Martian surface, or violently sucking a neighboring star's gases into a black hole. And recall that more than a hundred chemical compounds of carbon, oxygen, and other elements have been found in space and in meteorites, including complex molecules of amino acids. That is clear evidence that Earthlike chemical processes are common beyond Earth. This means that we can expect to find certain general chemical and biological similarities on planets of other stars.

For example, since hydrogen by far is the most abundant element in the Universe, we can expect hydrogen to be an important component of living matter wherever life has evolved. Ices containing water also are common during planetary formation. Stellar energy and primitive organisms break down the water and so liberate its oxygen to the air. We could expect organisms on virtually any habitable planet to be capable of breaking down water molecules.

We could also expect to find certain general similarities among the organic molecules built up early in a habitable planet's life history, since water, ammonia, methane, and nitrogen, for example, are common ingredients in Earthlike planets. But exactly what happens to large organic molecules as they evolve chemically and then biologically over the first few millions of years, and then later, is impossible to say. The myriad pathways of chemical and biological evolution are far too numerous and complex. Of one thing we can be certain: Among a billion alien life forms there will be no salmon, squirrels, parrots, or people like us. As the late biologist Loren Eiseley in his book *The Immense Journey* so eloquently put it:

> Life, even cellular life, may exist out yonder in the dark. But high or low in nature, it will not wear the shape of man. That shape is the evolutionary product of a strange, long wandering through the attics of the forest roof, and so great are the chances of failure that nothing precisely and identically human is likely ever to come that way again.

> . . . Nowhere in all space or on a thousand worlds will there be men to share our loneliness. There may be wisdom; there may be power; somewhere across space great instruments, handled by strange manipulative organs, may stare vainly at our floating cloud wrack, their owners yearning as we yearn. Nevertheless, in the nature of life and in the principles of evolution we have had our answer. Of men elsewhere, and beyond, there will be none forever.

How to Find a Habitable Planet

The search for planets beyond the Sun, and for alien life forms, is not new. Nor are the reasons for searching. Astronomers have been peering into space with different kinds of instruments for many years, but it wasn't until 1995 that they began finding planets circling other stars. Astronomers, biologists, philosophers, theologians, and others consider the discovery of planetary systems beyond our own important. We can observe many stars in different stages of formation, from their birth in their dark nebula stellar nurseries through middle age, and finally to a violent or peaceful farewell. Such studies of other stars are teaching us much about the Sun. But this has not yet happened with planets. The discovery of other planetary systems now being formed, or formed a few billion years ago, will teach us about our own Solar System. The more such planetary systems we can find and study, the more we will know about the ways planets are formed, including Earth and its companions.

INDIRECT AND DIRECT SEARCHES

Astronomers learn about the stars by studying their light. By analyzing a star's ray of light through instruments called spectroscopes, we can tell in which direction the star is moving, the composition of its gases, its surface temperature, and other properties. Spectroscopes provide such information not only about nearby and distant stars, but also about the most distant galaxies we can see. But visible light gives us only a narrow glimpse of the broad energy spectrum of a star. We can pry out still more stellar secrets by "viewing" a star with special instruments in small space satellite observatories that we have put into orbit about Earth. Some of these instruments study a star's gamma ray emissions. Others look at stars through the X-ray window of the electromagnetic spectrum, and still others through the ultraviolet and radio wave windows.

So far in our search for other worlds, we have found planets orbiting three different Sunlike stars, and by the time you read this the list probably will have grown. In October 1995, Michel Mayor and Didier Queloz of the Geneva (Switzerland) Observatory announced that they had discovered a giant planet orbiting the star known as 51 Pegasi. And what a strange planet it turned out to be.

You can see 51 Pegasi through binoculars just to the right of the constellation the Great Square of Pegasus. Three months later the two American astronomers Geoffrey W. Marcy and R. Paul Butler discovered two more planets also circling Sunlike stars. One planet orbits the star 70 Virginis (in the constellation Virgo the Virgin). The other belongs to the star 47 Ursae Majoris (in the constellation Ursa Major the Great Bear). But no one has actually seen the planets. They are so close to their parent star that they are lost in its glare. It's like trying to photograph a firefly circling a giant searchlight. If we can't see them, then how do we know they are there? Their discovery involves the "indirect" method of planet search.

All four astronomers were not trying to spot a planet the way we spot a moon of Jupiter, for instance. Instead, they were looking for a wobble motion of the star. Imagine the case of the planet orbiting 70 Virginis. That planet turns out to be at least 6.5 times more massive than Jupiter. As it orbits the star, the star's gravity tugs on the planet and so keeps it in orbit. At the same time the planet's gravity also tugs on the star. The result is a wobble motion of the star. The more massive such a planet is, the stronger its gravitational tug on its star, and the greater the wobble pattern. The same is true in a double star system.

To detect a star's wobble, astronomers photograph the star through a spectroscope night after night, week after week, and sometimes year after year. In some cases, the resulting photographs can reveal an up-and-down wobble. That happens if we see the star tipped over on its side and its planet orbiting about the star's equator. In certain other cases the wobble will show a pattern of a slight movement first toward and then away from Earth. In such cases we are viewing the star and its planet just as we view Venus and Mercury orbiting the Sun. In both cases we can analyze the wobble pattern and work out the size and shape of the planet's orbit. We can also tell the mass of the planet.

How to Detect a Planet Orbiting a Distant Star

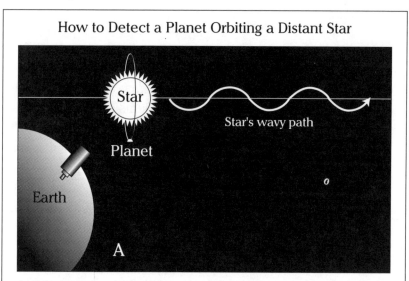

A. If a planet is orbiting a star in a vertical direction as seen from Earth, the planet's gravitational tug on the star will cause the star to follow a wavy path as we trace its motion across the sky.

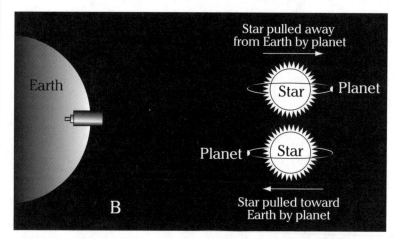

B. If a planet is orbiting a star in a horizontal direction as seen from Earth, the planet's gravitational tug on the star will cause the star to move toward us when the planet is between us and the star, and then move away from us when the planet is on the far side of the star.

NEW PLANETS POSE NEW MYSTERIES

The three "new" planets are rather different from each other and unlike anything seen before. At a distance of forty light-years from us, 51 Pegasi's planet is the oddest. It has a mass about half that of Jupiter and orbits its star at a sizzling distance of only 4.4 million miles (7 million kilometers), only one-eighth Mercury's close distance to the Sun. The surface temperature on the planet must be at least 1,800°F (1,000°C). A year for the planet equals just 4.2 Earth days, which means that every month on the planet you would be seven years older. The planet of 51 Pegasi clearly does not fall within our habitable zone, so it hardly qualifies as a life-supporting planet. Astronomers now wonder how such a massive planet could form so close to its local star. In the Solar System the large planets are the most distant.

What about the other two planets? 47 Ursae Majoris's planet has a year equal to three Earth years and lies some 186 million miles (300 million kilometers) from its star. That would put the planet in the middle of the asteroid belt between Mars and Jupiter if the planet were orbiting the Sun. Its mass is about 2.3 times greater than Jupiter's mass. If the planet were a member of the Solar System, it clearly would be considered a gas giant and not a likely candidate for Earth life. A planet that massive would make walking around very difficult, if it had a suitable surface to walk around on.

Marcy and Butler's other planet, around the star 70 Virginis, is very different from the other two. With an orbital period of 117 Earth days, it has a rather stretched-out orbit and has a mass 6.5 times that of Jupiter. Although it lies in its star's habitable zone, it fails to offer many prospects for life. First, it is an enormous gas giant most likely with a suffocating atmosphere. Second, it probably isn't a planet at all, but a brown dwarf instead.

Unfortunately, for now at least, we have only three extrasolar (meaning "beyond the Sun") planetary candidates for life. All three are giants and not very promising worlds for life forms that might walk, crawl, swim, or hop around, no matter what their shape or their biology. Why have we found only giant planets so far? Aren't there smaller, Earthlike planets out there also? There most probably are, and millions of them in our galaxy alone. The reason we are finding only giants as our search for extrasolar planets begins in earnest is that our search instruments can detect only "large" star wobbles. And large star wobbles are produced only by large planets. The smaller the planet, the smaller the wobble of its star, and the smaller the wobble the more difficult the motion is to detect. So for now at least, the limitations of our instruments place size limits on the extrasolar planets we are able to detect.

THE PROMISE OF A NEW KIND OF TELESCOPE

Earlier we said that the indirect, or wobble, method is the only one we presently have for discovering new planets. Also, the only properties of the planet it reveals are the planet's mass and orbit. It tells us nothing about its atmosphere, which is an important key to the kind of life, if any, the planet might harbor. At present, the direct method involves trying to spot that planetary firefly circling a powerful stellar searchlight, but we do not yet have instruments capable of peering through a star's glare to spot a planet orbiting close by. However, that may soon change, and with promising results. It will mean reinventing the telescope, or rather designing and building a new kind of telescope.

And just that is now being done by a team of more than twenty scientists and engineers led by telescope designers J. Roger, P. Angel, and Neville J. Woolf of the Steward Observatory at the University of Arizona. The evolution of this remarkable telescope idea began around 1973.

Ronald N. Bracewell of Stanford University around that time reasoned that two small telescopes working together in a certain way should be able to photograph extrasolar planets, despite the glare of their parent star. The two telescopes spaced sixty-six feet (twenty meters) apart would be pointed at the target star, in effect sighting through a giant pair of binoculars. Photographing a star through both telescopes at once would, as expected, reveal the star as a single bright point of light. Knowing that light travels as waves, with the peaks and troughs similar to a train of ocean waves, gave Bracewell an idea. He would arrange one telescope in such a way that it turned the wave train of light upside down, so that the peaks were flipped over as troughs and the troughs as peaks. Then he would combine the upside-down light train from the star with the right-side-up light train from the other telescope. When exactly overlapped, the two light trains should cancel each other out and the star dim to a mere ghost image. It worked.

But why go to the trouble of focusing on a star, getting a sharp view of it, and then canceling out its light? If the star had a planet, the planet would pop into view the instant the star's light was masked. Suddenly the firefly-planet would blink on when the searchlight-star blinked off. The planet would become visible because it was offset from the star.

Bracewell's two-telescope instrument is called an *interferometer* because it involves the interference of trains of light waves. At the beach you sometimes see two small trains of ocean waves coming from two different directions near the shore, meeting, and so interfering with each other. As they merge, the crests of one wave train flow across the troughs of the other wave train, and the waves dissolve.

In theory, Bracewell's idea works. The heat of the reflected light from the distant planet is detected as infrared "light" by the telescope. But in practice there are two problems: 1) Telescopes based on the ground cannot tell the infrared energy of the distant planet from infrared energy given off by the space dust particles that cause the zodiacal light glow. Furthermore, Earth's atmosphere blocks most of the infrared energy striking it. 2) No interferometer can perfectly cancel out all the light from a star. That means that a dim planet close to a target star could still be lost in the star's slight glare. So what to do?

Angel's group seems to have come up with ways to solve both problems. To avoid, or at least minimize, space dust, they would put the interferometer assembly of four telescopes in space, but not in an orbit around Earth where the Hubble Space Telescope is. In Earth orbit the interferometer would receive confusing heat signals from our planet. It would have to be put in an orbit around the Sun out at Jupiter's distance. That would keep the telescope "cool" by protecting it from the infrared energy radiated into space by Earth. From that distance the background glare of zodiacal dust would also diminish. Further, with the background dust glare diminished, the size of the four telescopes could be reduced from the original twenty-six feet (eight meters) each to only 3.3 feet (1 meter) in diameter. Angel says the telescope design is so good that if the instrument were pointed at the Solar System from the distance of a nearby star, it would block out the Sun's light so well that it could pick out Venus, Earth, Mars, Jupiter, and Saturn. If the telescope were in space today, it could easily study the planet around 47 Ursae Majoris.

For many, the most remarkable thing about the telescope is that it would be able to examine the atmosphere of its target planet and detect signs of life. Supposing that the life forms were not advanced enough to send out radio signals to announce their existence, they would reveal themselves in other ways. For example, large amounts of oxygen in a planet's atmosphere could indicate some form of carbon-based life. Additionally, carbon dioxide, methane, and water in an alien atmosphere could be picked up. The presence of large amounts of oxygen by itself need not necessarily point to its production by life forms. The oxygen might have a simple chemical (nonbiological) source. Also, life on an alien world might have a chemical system that does not produce oxygen as carbon-based life does. But we now risk entering the realm of science-fiction. Knowing that the laws of physics and chemistry familiar to us on Earth have been demonstrated time and again to operate beyond Earth, it seems reasonable for us to expect life on another planet to have a chemistry at least resembling our own, if not an exact copy.

Says Angel, "The discovery of life on another planet could be the crowning achievement in the exploration of space. . . . Remarkably, the technology to assist in this discovery is at our fingertips."

8 ▼

AS THE SUN DIES

For more than three billion years, species have come and gone, unwitting subjects of nature's grandest experiment—evolution. Successful for a cosmic while, multitudes have then been snuffed out time and again. The agent of those mass killings has been some environmental quirk of nature spawned by an erratic Sun or by Earth's ever-changing orbit, internal rumblings, or climate change as the planet has been battered and dented by asteroid and comet impacts.

Earth's ultimate fate, however, lies not with the coming and going of species, or with calamitous rains of asteroids and comets. It lies with the long-term future of our principal provider, the Sun. Like all stars, the Sun must one day go out and stop powering Earth's three main life-support systems—global circulation of the atmosphere, the planet's vast store of liquid water, and its cover of green plants, which are the basic food for virtually all organisms. It has been only since the 1960s or so that astronomers have come to learn enough about the internal workings of Sunlike stars to predict their demise. Among such astronomers are I. -Juliana Sackmann, Arnold I. Boothroyd, and Kathleen E. Kraemer.

THE BEGINNING OF THE END

In chapter 4 we left the Sun as a fully formed star shining as we see it today by burning its hydrogen fuel in the nuclear furnace of its central core. The extremely high pressure and temperature created in the core region by the overlying weight of gases fuse the vast store of hydrogen nuclei into helium. With a trillion such fusion reactions taking place each second, a small amount of hydrogen mass is converted into a relatively large amount of energy. It is that relationship between small mass loss and great energy production that enables the Sun to shine over its life span of about 10 billion years as the yellowish-white star we see today. Astronomers call that stage of the Sun its *main sequence* life. Since the Sun has been burning for nearly five billion years as a main sequence star, the question we must now ask is what happens in another five or six billion years when the core hydrogen fuel has been used up?

In any star that shines more or less steadily, as the Sun does, a tug of war rages between gravity and pressure. Gravity causes the entire mass of the star to try to tumble into the core region. That, by the way, is why massive objects like stars and planets are shaped as a sphere rather than as an Idaho potato. Meanwhile, pressure within the core generated by high temperature pushes outward just enough to balance the gravitational infall of the star's upper layers. As long as nobody wins the tug of war, the star shines more or less steadily.

In the short run, pressure sometimes wins, then gravity takes its turn. But these are brief bouts. A star's nuclear furnace sometimes burns hot, then it may burn somewhat cooler for a while. During these stages, the star balloons out and then shrinks, brightens and then fades for a while in lazy pulses.

On the whole, however, the Sun seems to have been ever so gradually brightening over its main sequence stage and expanding a bit, and astronomers expect the brightening and expanding to continue. The reason is that the ever-changing makeup of the core requires an ever-higher temperature to keep the pressure high. The young main-sequence Sun was probably some thirty percent dimmer than it is today. And today it seems to be about ten percent larger. As a result, Earth life will not have the privilege of carrying on for the additional six billion years of the Sun's main-sequence life. The end will come much sooner, in only a bit more than one billion years from now. By that time the Sun's total energy output will be some ten percent higher than it is today.

Ten percent may not sound like much, but that increase in energy output will be devastating for life on Earth, according to astronomer James F. Kasting. He expects the brightening to trigger a runaway greenhouse effect on Earth. And if intelligent beings still inhabit the planet by that time, they will be helpless to prevent it. Gradually the planet will begin to lose its water through evaporation. The resulting cloud cover created by all that evaporation may delay things for a short while by blocking much of the Sun's radiation from reaching the ground. But sooner or later, life as we know it will no longer be possible.

Some 300 million years later the oceans will be hot enough to boil and evaporate away. Although that time will mark the end of life on the planet, it will not mark the end of the planet's physical evolution. The continuing churning of magma deep within Earth will keep reshaping its unbearably hot surface by pushing and crunching its plates this way and that as in the past. The vast expanse of now-exposed ocean bottom, with trenches that could swallow Earth's highest mountains, and old worn-off flat-topped volcanic peaks would offer a strange sight. Earth's surface in 3.5 billion years probably will resemble that of Venus today. As we'll find in a moment, that distant year, although a dismal one for Earth, might mark the beginnings of life on one or more moons of the gas-giant planets Jupiter and Saturn.

We now move the geological clock ahead some 4.8 billion years to the time the Sun will be 9.4 billion years old. That day marks a major event in the Sun's life—its core hydrogen fuel tank runs dry. The Sun must now switch to a shell region just outside the core where its nuclear fires can continue to burn hydrogen. This marks the end of the Sun as a main-sequence star and its beginning as a red giant.

The "reserve" supply of shell hydrogen fuel will not last very long. As it burns over the next 1.6 billion years, the cooling core gradually shrinks. The Sun is now 11 billion years old and well into its evolution as a red giant star, a terrorist of the Universe. Over the next 700 million years, the increasingly hot-burning hydrogen-shell region expands the Sun to seventy percent of its original size as a main-sequence star. Pressure, for a while, wins the tug of war with gravity and continues to puff the Sun up into an enormous sphere. Even though it blazes more than twice as hot as we see it today, its expanded outer gases are spread out so thinly that they glow with a cool red light. But a still hotter red-giant future awaits it. By now all of the former core hydrogen has been changed to helium—a new kind of fuel about to be ignited.

Before the Sun reaches the age of 12 billion years, it steadily increases in brightness, first to seventeen times brighter than today, then to thirty-four times. At age 12.2 billion years, the Sun's energy output soars to a staggering 2,300 times its brightness today. The Sun spends 600 million years in the first of its two red-giant stages. All the while it expands, until it is finally a raging swollen sphere about eighty times bigger than it is now. Its surface gases fill the Solar System out beyond the present orbit of Venus, three-quarters of the way to Earth's present orbit. As they do, they engulf and vaporize Mercury. In the process of swelling, the Sun throws off great puffs of its outer gas layers, discarding possibly a quarter or more of its mass.

With less mass than before, something interesting happens. The Sun's gravitational pull on the remaining planets weakens. The rule in the Universe is that the more mass an object has, the stronger its gravitational pull. With a weakened gravitational grip acting on them, Venus, Earth, and the other planets begin to spiral outward and settle into new and more distant orbits. Venus escapes Mercury's fate of incineration by moving out to the present distance of Earth's orbit. Meanwhile, Earth spirals out to more than half again its present distance from the Sun.

While hydrogen is burning in the shell around the helium core, the core continues to collapse and so heats up. Eventually, the core temperature reaches 100,000,000 K and the core pressure quadruples. At this point the core helium—"ash" from the original core fusions of hydrogen—ignites as fuel for a new set of fusion reactions. The helium is now hot enough to begin fusing into the heavier elements carbon and oxygen. As it ignites, there is a "helium flash." When the core next heats up and expands, the new outburst of energy never reaches the Sun's surface. The reason is that the core also expands and cools the hydrogen-burning shell. The result is a dimming of the Sun's surface brightness to about half, and the gradual shrinking of the Sun from its red-giant size. The dimming takes about 10,000 years.

Over the next million years or so of adjustment to its new core conditions, the Sun pulses brighter, then dimmer, and then brighter again. Eventually, it settles down and for the next 100 million years shines steadily as a helium-burner. But because the shell hydrogen also continues to burn, the Sun becomes a double burner, which causes it to blaze away about 44 times hotter than it does today and with a diameter five times greater than now.

Some 12.3 billion years from now, the Sun exhausts its core helium fuel. In place of the used-up helium is a core of mostly carbon. The dying Sun lacks the mass needed to push the core temperature and pressure high enough to fuse the carbon. No Sunlike star can. Except for the outer shell of hydrogen, which continues to burn, the Sun's last supply of usable fuel is the helium in a shell just outside the carbon core. When the shell helium ignites, a new burst of energy once again expands the Sun's outer gas layers, and it enters its second life as a red giant. This time it balloons out to ninety times its present diameter. Its surface gases swell out nearly to Earth's present orbit. But by now Earth has long been gone in a new orbit 1.7 times larger than before.

Because the Sun's core is no longer burning, the core pressure drops and the core shrinks. As it does, it causes a squeezing of both the outer hydrogen-burning shell and the inner helium-burning shell just outside the core. The squeezing triggers a final series of solar outbursts in the form of at least four new helium flashes that boost the Sun's total energy output a million times. The first flash takes some 10,600 years to complete and swells the Sun up 106 times its present diameter so that it fills space all the way out to Earth's present orbit. The Sun then shrinks down to about a quarter its previous size. A second flash erupts a hundred thousand years later and again puffs up the Sun four times larger. In all, the four flashes take place over 400,000 years. Depending on how much mass the Sun casts off during its second red-giant stage and after, there could be a grand outburst of up to 10 helium flashes, like the final explosive display at a fourth of July fireworks festival.

A hundred thousand years after its last helium flash, the Sun casts off all its outer gas layers as a planetary nebula. Only the core remains exposed. We can see older Sunlike stars now undergoing just such mass loss. The Sun shrinks to an object only 50,000 miles (80,000 kilometers) in diameter. It has no way to generate more energy by nuclear fusions. Its usable hydrogen is all gone, as is its usable helium. Gravity now takes over and wins the tug of war with pressure. The Sun simply keeps shrinking. As it does, the tremendous amount of heat and other stored energy has a smaller and smaller surface area from which to shine. The result is a tremendously hot surface.

As a middle-aged star, the Sun's surface gases burned a yellowish white at 6,000 K. As a red giant, its cooler surface gases burned red at about 4,000 K. Some hundred thousand years after the last helium flash, the shrunken star's hot surface glows white-hot at 120,000 K. The Sun becomes a white dwarf star only half as massive as before and shrunken down to about the size of Earth. It is now some 12.4 billion years old. The Sun will keep shining for billions of years, but only with the stored heat left over from earlier days of fusion reactions. Unable to fuse its carbon core into heavier elements, and with its hydrogen and helium shells dead, the Sun can only grow cooler and dimmer over that seeming eternity, eventually growing cold and fading to a black dwarf.

FINAL FATE OF THE PLANETS

What of Earth and the other planets during the Sun's final days? When the Sun shed another eighteen percent of its mass in its second red giant stage, its gravitational pull was further weakened. Earth and its siblings once again spiraled still farther away from their dying parent star. They then remained in those final orbits through the Sun's long term as a white dwarf. But even later, as a black-dwarf relic, the Sun still has enough mass to keep its children in tow. And one of those children is Earth, now a dead, shrunken, and frozen world, for its own internal fires cooled long ago—a burned-out cinder.

The astronomers who wrote this story of the Sun's long-term

future cannot, of course, be certain that the Sun's end will come exactly as they predict. But based on what we know about the Sun today, and what we can observe about other Sunlike stars—some younger, others older—their model seems possible. One of the many details the designers of the solar model cannot be sure about is just how much mass the Sun will lose during its two red-giant stages. If the mass loss is much less than the astronomers think it may be, then the Sun will not let its planets stray quite so far from their present orbits. There would also be an estimated ten helium flashes at the end. As Mercury was gobbled up earlier, so would Venus be engulfed, but not until the second helium flash. Earth would be incinerated during the fifth flash. The Sun would then swell to its largest size on the seventh flash, ballooning out a bit more than half again the present distance of Earth's orbit. Because Mars by then will have spiraled out into an orbit 2.25 times Earth's present distance from the Sun, Mars would be spared a fiery death, but barely so.

What of the planets beyond Mars? They, too, will have spiraled outward a bit into safer orbits. The moons of the gas-giant planets would be warmed enough for their icy crusts to melt as liquid water. Some of those moons might even find themselves in a habitable life zone.

At the present time the large moons of the gas giant planets are too far from the Sun to be warmed by solar radiation. So they remain icy worlds. But photographs taken by the *Voyager* and *Galileo* space crafts strongly hint that liquid water flows beneath those cracked and streaked crusts of ice. The energy that keeps the water liquid probably comes from heat produced by the decay of radioactive elements deep within the moons. It also comes from two other activities: 1) frictional heating caused by the churning of the moons' hot rocky or metal cores; and 2) tidal heating caused when ground tides, not unlike ocean tides, are raised on the moons by the gravity of the massive planets they orbit.

Photographs of these icy worlds strongly hint of recent activity at the surface and beneath. Jupiter's moon Europa, for instance, appears free of the many impact craters found on most of the moons of the Solar System. The icy crust is also broken into large pieces like those of a jigsaw puzzle. It now seems likely that tidal forces acting on the moon squeeze water or soft ice up through cracks between the pieces from time to time. Dark material then appears within the cracks. Many of the cracks seem recent, others much older. There are even blocks of ice that seem to be floating about. Galileo's orbital action around Europa leads astronomers to suspect that the moon has a solid core about as dense as Earth's. Surrounding the core may be a mantle of rock above which is a layer of water or soft ice.

Some planetary scientists suspect that the dark matter filling some of the cracks is carbon-rich organic material. They even envision warm, mineral-rich geysers issuing from the ocean-bottom rock deep beneath. Many such hot outpourings from Earth's ocean bottom have been discovered in recent years, and the regions teem with life. Where there is a mix of organic molecules and warm water, it now seems there can be life.

Another candidate for the chemical evolution of life is Jupiter's moon Ganymede. It is the largest moon in the Solar System, with a diameter of 3,280 miles (5,275 kilometers). Gravity measurements, along with the strength of the moon's magnetic field, make astronomers think that the large moon has a metal core. Above the core may be a 500-mile

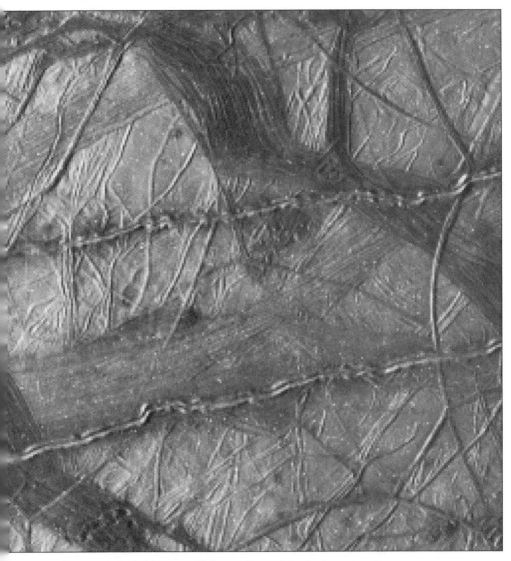

Fractures and ridges mark the surface of Jupiter's moon Europa, as photographed by the Galileo space probe in 1996. The area shown is about he distance from Los Angeles to San Diego, California—150 miles (240 kilometers). The dark bands suggest that the surface crust has been split and filled in with material welling up from inside the moon. NASA

Parallel ridges and troughs are the main surface features of Jupiter's moon Ganymede, as photographed by the Galileo space probe in 1996. Features as small as 250 feet (75 meters) can be made out. The photo was taken from a distance of 4,600 miles (7,400 kilometers) above Ganymede's surface. NASA

(800-kilometer) shell of rock topped by a 500-mile thickness of ice. Much of the satellite's mass seems to be water, and like Europa, its icy crust is laced with cracks, lanes, and mountainous ridges hundreds of miles long. But there are no craters, again suggesting that the moon's surface features are relatively new. Perhaps Ganymede also harbors warm, mineral-rich waters in which chemical evolution has already sparked primitive life forms. At this stage we simply don't know, but we can't resist wondering.

We can also wonder about Saturn's moon Enceladus and Neptune's satellite Triton, which seems to have an active interior. Saturn's largest moon, Titan, has an atmosphere even denser than Earth's. Solar wind particles that rain down through the atmosphere split molecules of nitrogen and methane. The nitrogen, carbon, and hydrogen atoms then recombine as large organic molecules that are heavy enough to rain out of the atmosphere onto the surface. A very similar process went on in Earth's early atmosphere. Although it is too cold for that rich store of organic molecules to do much of anything but sit there, 11 billion years from now a red giant Sun may change all that. While the inner planets are being vaporized or baked, the distant moons of the gas giant planets may be transformed into oases of evolution. Chemical evolution may have the opportunity to take off explosively, spawning life forms that will evolve and take their turn to bask for a while in the Sun.

But life on those moons so distant in space and time may not have the years needed to climb very high on the evolutionary tree. Remember, it took Earth life nearly four billion years to produce elephants and oak trees. Who can tell what shape a Titan forest may take, or what kinds of creatures high or low may roam those forests? Right now our knowledge is too meager to let us do more than wonder, and hope that somehow, somewhere a new chain of life may arise and continue in its turn. But after an evolutionary while, that life chain, too, will be doomed to extinction, not by fire but by ice as the red giant Sun shrinks to a white dwarf and the white dwarf cools and ultimately freezes.

With a retinue of perhaps a half-dozen frozen planetary hulks, the black-dwarf Sun will continue its journey through the darkness of galactic space. For eons uncountable it will circle the hub of the Milky Way in the company of countless other dead stars like it. By that time the Galaxy itself will be a large place of dying. Although some star formation will continue here and there, for the most part the Galaxy will be a dark place, lighted so faintly that it may be invisible to its neighbors, a Los Angeles in an ultimate power failure. However, since the rule seems to be that planets often form right along with new stars, some of the dying Galaxy's new planets may in their turn spawn strange and marvelous life forms of their own that will enjoy a place in their Suns, however briefly, on the cosmic time scale.

BEFORE EARTH BURNS

Before this inevitable scenario plays out, Earth's latter-day human species may see the end coming. And before it is too late, perhaps they will undertake the enormous task of abandoning a doomed planet and colonizing a habitable one belonging to a young and nearby Sunlike star.

Such notions may seem remote and farfetched, but they are not unbelievable. We have had our answer. It lies in the myriad stars we marvel at and study nightly and in which we are able to read unmistakably the life story of our local star, the Sun. But there is still much time, more than most of us could even hope for, to live a billion billion lives and for the Sun to continue to nourish Earth and its marvelously diverse inhabitants for more time than we can meaningfully count.

FURTHER READING

Angel, J. Roger P., and Neville J. Woolf, "Searching for Life on Other Planets," *Scientific American*, pp. 60–66, April 1996.

Bahcall, John N., "The Solar-Neutrino Problem," *Scientific American*, pp. 54–61, May 1990.

Baliunas, Sally, and Willie Soon, "The Sun-Climate Connection," *Sky & Telescope*, pp. 38–41, December 1996.

Black, David C., "Other Suns, Other Planets?" *Sky & Telescope*, pp. 20–27, August 1996.

Boothroyd, Arnold I., I.-Juliana Sackmann, and William A. Fowler, "Our Sun II: Early Mass Loss of 0.1 Solar Mass and the Case of the Missing Lithium," *The Astrophysical Journal*, 377: pp. 318–329, August 10, 1991.

Bracewell, Ronald N., *Intelligent Life in Outer Space*, San Francisco: W. H. Freeman, 1975.

——————, "Worlds Around Other Stars," *Scientific American*, pp. 76–82, January 1991

——————, "A Profusion of Planets," *The Sciences*, pp. 30–35, May/June 1989.

Browne, Malcolm W., "New Look at Apocalypse: Dying Sun Will Boil Seas and Leave Orbiting Cinder," *The New York Times*, pp. B5 and B9, September 20, 1994.

Cowen, Ron, "The Once and Future Sun," *Science News*, pp. 204–205, March 26, 1994.

——————, "New Crowd at the Solar System's Edge," *Science News*, p. 364, June 14, 1997.

——————, "Galileo Explores the Galilean Moons," *Science News*, pp. 90–91, August 9, 1997.

——————, "Spacecraft probes beneath sun's surface," *Science News*, p. 150, September 6, 1977.

Crawford, Ian, "How Common Are Technological Civilizations?" *Astronomy & Geophysics* (Royal Astronomical Society), pp. 24–26, August/September 1997.

Dole, Stephen H., *Habitable Planets for Man*, New York: Blaisdell, 1970.

Eddy, John A., "The Case of the Missing Sunspots," *Scientific American*, p. 80, May 1977.

Eicher, David J., "Ashes to Ashes and Dust to Dust," *Astronomy*, pp. 40–47, May 1994.

Foukal, Peter V., "The Variable Sun," *Scientific American*, pp. 34–41, February 1990.

Friedman, Herbert, *Sun and Earth*, Scientific American Books, 1986.

Gallant, Roy A., *Beyond Earth: the Search for Extraterrestrial Life*, Four Winds Press, 1977.

Gilfillan, Edward S., Jr., *Migration to the Stars*, Washington, D. C.: Robert B. Luce Co., 1975.

Graedel, T. E., I.-Juliana Sackmann, and A. I. Boothroyd, "Early Solar Mass Loss: A Potential Solution to the Weak Sun Paradox," *Geophysical Research Letters*, Vol. 18, No. 10, pp. 1881–1884, October 1991.

Hathaway, David H., "Journey to the Heart of the Sun," *Astronomy*, pp. 38–43, January 1995.

Kaler, James B., "Extreme Stars," *Astronomy*, pp. 54–59, January 1997.

Kennedy, James R., "GONG: Probing the Sun's Hidden Heart," *Sky & Telescope*, pp. 20–24, October 1996.

Lang, Kenneth R., "Unsolved Mysteries of the Sun—Part 1," *Sky & Telescope*, pp. 38–42, August 1996.

_____, "Unsolved Mysteries of the Sun—Part 2," *Sky & Telescope*, pp. 24–28, September 1996.

LIFE IN THE UNIVERSE. Special issue of *Scientific American*, October 1994.

MacRobert, Alan M., and Joshua Roth, "The Planet of 51 Pegasi," *Sky & Telescope*, pp. 38–40, January 1996.

Monastersky, Richard, "Reflections on a sunnier past," *Science News*, p. 287, November 2, 1991.

Pendleton, Yvonne J., and Jack D. Farmer, "Life: a cosmic imperative?" *Sky & Telescope*, pp. 42–47, July 1997.

Sackmann, I.-Juliana, Arnold I. Boothroyd, and Kathleen E. Kraemer, "Our Sun III: Present and Future," *The Astrophysical Journal*, 418: pp. 457–468, November 20, 1993.

––––––––––, and William A. Fowler, "Our Sun I: the Standard Mode—Successes and Failures," *The Astrophysical Journal*, 360: pp. 727–736, September 10, 1990.

Sagan, Carl, *The Cosmic Connection, an Extraterrestrial Perspective*, New York: Dell Publishing Co., 1973.

Stephens, Sally, "Excesses of Youth," *Astronomy*, pp. 36–41, September 1996.

Thompson, Dick, "Eyes on the Storm-Tossed Sun," *Time*, pp. 68– 69, September 8, 1997.

Wakefield, Julie, "Cosmic Rain," *Sky & Telescope*, pp. 29–30, August, 1997.

GLOSSARY

amino acids—complex molecules that were among the first molecules of life nearly four billion years ago. They contain carbon, oxygen, nitrogen, and hydrogen. The building blocks of proteins, there are about twenty different kinds of amino acids.

asteroid—any of millions of rock-metal fragments ranging in size from a football to hundreds of miles across and traveling about the Sun in orbits predominantly lying between Mars and Jupiter. Now and then an asteroid may be gravitationally disturbed and flung off into a new orbit that may take it relatively close to Earth or another planet.

atom—the smallest possible piece of an element (see **element**) that can take part in a chemical reaction. An atom retains all the properties of its element.

big bang—the theory of the beginning of time and the Universe between twelve billion and twenty billion years ago, marked by the fireball-explosion of a tiny pinpoint of mass, a kind of super-atom that contained all the mass and energy the Universe was to have.

black dwarf—a star that has passed through the white dwarf stage and is radiating so little energy that it can no longer be observed directly.

black hole—an incredibly dense and massive star that has burned itself out. Black holes are thought to be so dense that radiation is unable to escape from them; hence, we know of no way of observing them directly.

blue giant—an especially massive, large, and luminous star that is seen to shine with a bluish-white light. The core temperatures and surface temperatures of these short-lived stars are many times higher than those of less massive stars such as the Sun.

brown dwarf—objects with too little mass to become stars that radiate energy by nuclear fusions. They are approximately midway between Jupiter and the smallest true stars in mass. They probably exist throughout the galaxies by the millions. Most are so far away and so dim that detecting them is very difficult, although the Hubble Space Telescope has detected them.

chromosphere—the Sun's lower atmosphere lying between the corona and the photosphere surface layer of gases. The temperature of the chromosphere is some ten thousand kelvins. The term means "color sphere." During a solar eclipse the chromosphere is seen as a thin pink rim circling the darkened solar disk.

comet—a loose swarm of ices and carbon and silicate dust that travels around the Sun in a long elliptical orbit. The visible part of a comet consists of a gas envelope called the coma, a dense central nucleus, and usually a tail millions of miles long. Some comets reappear regularly while others appear only once, but both eventually break up or leave the Solar System. The storehouse of comets is the Oort Cloud, a spherical collection of the ice balls lying at a radius of more than a trillion miles from the Sun.

convective zone—that zone within the Sun located beneath the photosphere and above the radiative zone. Conveyor belt-like cells of convective zone gases transfer heat from the radiative zone up into the photosphere.

corona—the Sun's outermost layer of atmospheric gases that appear as a feathery display during a solar eclipse. At a temperature of millions of kelvins, the corona expands to become the solar wind.

eccentricity—that property of a planet's orbit that characterizes the degree of elongation of the orbit; for example, the highly eccentric orbit of Pluto is stretched out as a long ellipse, whereas Earth's nearly circular orbit is of low eccentricity.

electromagnetic spectrum—the range of energy typically emitted by stars. The shortest and most energetic wavelengths are gamma rays. Then at increasingly longer wavelengths come x-rays, ultraviolet energy, visible light, infrared radiation, microwave radiation, and radio waves.

electron—a negative unit of electricity and part of all atoms. Clouds of electrons surround the nuclei of atoms. The mass of an electron is only a small fraction of the mass of a proton (1/1,840 that of the hydrogen atom).

element—a substance made up entirely of the same kinds of atoms. Such a substance cannot be broken down into a simpler substance by chemical means. Examples of elements are carbon, gold, oxygen, lead, chlorine.

eruptive variable stars—variable stars that increase in brightness as a result of exploding mildly or catastrophically.

faculae—bright patches within the Sun's photosphere seen in association with sunspots. The term means "little torches."

foraminifera—fossil shells of tiny marine organisms that lived millions of years ago and that can be analyzed to reveal the temperatures of ancient seas.

flash stars—variable red dwarf stars that flash into brightness and remain bright from a few minutes up to three hours. Several flash stars are in the Pleiades star cluster and may be new stars in the process of heating up.

fusion—a nuclear reaction process that produces energy in stars by transforming hydrogen into helium, and helium into heavier elements. Elements with atomic weight up to but not heavier than iron can be produced by nuclear fusion reactions.

galaxy—a vast collection of stars, gas, and dust held together gravitationally. Spiral galaxies, the brightest galaxies known, have a dense nucleus of stars with less dense spiral arms. Our galaxy, the Milky Way, is a spiral galaxy containing 300 billion or more stars.

granules—the lumpy appearance of the Sun's photosphere, or outer "surface" layer of gases, due to upwellings of hotter gases from lower depths cooling at differing rates as they rise above the photosphere surface.

greenhouse effect—the heat-trapping action of the atmosphere due to the blocking of long-wave radiation reflected from Earth's surface.

greenhouse gases—gases that contribute to the greenhouse effect and that include carbon dioxide, chlorofluorocarbons, nitrous oxide, methane, and water vapor.

habitable zone—the range of distance from a star within which conditions on a planet are favorable enough to permit the enormous variety of chemical reactions that lead to the origin and evolution of living matter.

interferometer—an instrument that causes light waves to interfere with each other and that measures wavelength and velocity.

isotope—atoms of the same element that have different atomic weights, although they have the same atomic number. If an element has three isotopes, each isotope will have exactly the same arrangement of electrons and exactly the same number of protons, but have a different number of neutrons, and hence different atomic weights. The ninety elements occurring in nature have more than three hundred isotopes.

Kuiper belt—that region of space beyond Pluto where comets are stored and from which cometary matter occasionally escapes and enters the inner Solar System, named after the American astronomer, Gerard Kuiper.

light-minute—the distance that light travels in one minute at the rate of 186,000 miles per second (300,000 kilometers), which amounts to 11,160,000 miles (17,960,000 kilometers). Earth is approximately eight light-minutes from the Sun.

light-year (l. y.)—the distance that light travels in one year, at the rate of 186,000 miles per second (300,000 kilometers), which is about six trillion miles (ten trillion kilometers).

Maunder sunspot minimum—the seventy-year period ending in 1715 in which fewer sunspots were observed than English astronomer E. Walter Maunder found to be the "normal" Sun's production of sunspots in one year. This discovery revealed that the Sun goes through periods of higher and lower activity.

meteoroid—any one of various rock and/or metal fragments orbiting the Sun singly or in swarms. As these objects enter Earth's atmosphere, they either burn up completely and exhibit streaks of light (as meteors), or their remains may fall to the ground as meteorites.

Milankovitch cycles—three major Earth rhythms proposed in the 1930s by the Yugoslavian geophysicist Milutin Milankovitch to induce climate change—precession, variation in the planet's obliquity, and the slow periodic change in the shape of Earth's orbit.

nebula—a great cloud of dust and gas within a galaxy. Some nebulae (reflection nebulae) reflect light generated by nearby stars, or by stars embedded within the nebula. Others (dark nebulae) are dark. Still others (emission nebulae) reradiate energy emitted by stars embedded within them. And still others (so called planetary nebulae) take the form of a great shell of gas cast off by an eruptive, or explosive, star.

neutrino—a subatomic particle with no electric charge and regarded as having hardly any, or no, mass, produced during nuclear fusions within the Sun's core.

neutron—a subatomic particle with no electrical charge. Neutrons are contained in the nuclei of all atoms, except hydrogen. They are only slightly more massive than protons. Outside the atom, neutrons have a life of only twenty minutes or so before they decompose into an electron and a proton and give off gamma rays.

neutron stars—stars made up of neutrons. Because neutrons are without an electrical charge and there is no force of repulsion, they can be packed very closely together. Consequently, neutron stars are extremely dense objects.

nova—a star that, for some reason not yet fully understood, bursts into brilliance. Within a few days a typical nova may become hundreds or thousands of times brighter than usual, then it becomes somewhat less brilliant, and after a few months or longer the star returns to its pre-nova brightness. Certain planetary nebulae may be the result of nova eruptions.

nuclear fusion—the process by which the Sun and other stars generate energy by fusing hydrogen nuclei into the nuclei of helium and elements as heavy as carbon (in Sunlike stars) or as heavy as iron (in gigantic stars).

nucleus—in astronomy, the central portion of a galaxy or a comet. In chemistry and physics, the central portion of an atom. In biology, the central region of a cell.

obliquity—the degree to which a planet's polar axis is inclined to the plane of its orbit. Earth's obliquity is 23.5 degrees.

paleoclimatologist—a scientist who studies ancient climates.

photosphere—the Sun's outer layer of "surface" gases that appear a dull yellowish-white and glow at a temperature of about 6,000 kelvins.

planet—a celestial object that shines by reflected light from a star about which the planet is held gravitationally captive and about which it revolves.

planetary nebula—a nebula such as the Ring Nebula in the constellation Lyra, once mistakenly thought to be a planet. Their faint greenish color gives them the appearance of the planet Uranus. (See also **nebulae**.)

planetesimals—rock, metal, and icy debris out of which the planets formed by gravitational accretion some 4.6 billion years ago.

positron—a positively charged electron that has the same mass but opposite charge of an electron.

proton—a positively charged subatomic particle found in the nuclei of all atoms. A proton's positive charge is equal in strength to the negative charge of an electron, but a proton is 1,840 times more massive than an electron. (See also **electron**.)

protoplanet—during the formation of the Solar System, any accumulation of matter from the solar disk that gravitationally swept up increasing amounts of mass, resulting in the formation of a planet.

protostar—a newly forming star that has not yet begun to radiate visible energy as a result of fusing hydrogen nuclei into helium nuclei in the star's core region. (See also **nuclear fusion**.)

pulsar—a rapidly rotating neutron star that sends out pulses of radiation. When the radiation is emitted in the direction of Earth, we receive pulses in lighthouse fashion. About 150 or so pulsars have been detected; each has its own rate of pulsation.

radiative zone—that zone within the Sun beneath the convective zone and above the Sun's core. One of the functions of this zone is the insulation against heat loss from the core.

red dwarf—a star with relatively little mass and a low surface temperature (about 3,000 kelvins), which causes the star to shine with a cool reddish light.

red giant—an enormous star that shines with a reddish light because of its relatively low surface temperature (about 3,000 kelvins). It is now thought that most stars go through a red-giant stage after they exhaust their core hydrogen and the core collapses gravitationally. The star then swells up and becomes a red giant.

scintillation—the twinkling appearance of stars due to motion of the atmosphere through which we view the stars.

spicule—an upward surging needle of gases occurring at the base of the chromosphere. Spicules form and dissolve in a continuous process.

solar wind—streams of charged particles (protons and electrons) emitted by the Sun. The solar wind sweeps throughout the Solar System and is especially strong when the Sun is most active.

star—a hot glowing globe of gas that emits energy all along the electromagnetic spectrum. The Sun is a typical star, and our closest. Most stars are enormous compared with planets, containing enough matter to make thousands of Earths. Stars generate energy by the fusion of atomic nuclei in their dense and hot cores. Stars seem to be formed out of clouds of gas and dust, evolve through various stages, and finally end their lives as dark, cold objects called black dwarfs.

sunspots—dark-appearing patches visible from time to time in the Sun's photosphere. They occur most frequently between five degrees and thirty five degrees north and south of the Sun's equator and range in size from a few hundred miles in diameter to diameters larger than Earth's. They appear dark because their eruptions send their gases high above the Sun's "surface," where they cool and so appear darker than the lower and hotter surface gases. Sunspots signal solar activity that causes auroral displays in Earth's atmosphere and may generate disruptions of radio and other electronic apparatus in Earth's environment, including the operation of artificial satellites.

supernova—a giant star whose brightness is tremendously increased by a catastrophic explosion. Supernova stars are many thousands of times brighter than ordinary nova stars. In a single second, a supernova releases as much energy as the Sun does over a period of about sixty years.

variable star—a star that periodically, and predictably, varies in brightness. It brightens and dims in cycles that repeat over periods of hours, months, or years.

white dwarf—an old and very small star that radiates stored energy rather than new energy generated through nuclear fusions. The Sun is destined to become a white dwarf after it goes through two red-giant stages and ends its life as an object about the size of Earth.

zodiacal light—a faint band of light stretching all along the ecliptic, or the plane of the planets' orbits, the brightest part being near the Sun. The light may be sunlight reflected by a disk of space matter (possibly small meteoroids) stretching out around the Sun. It is best seen in clear air late in the evening in March and September.

INDEX

Page numbers for illustrations are in **boldface**